Girls with Guns

A nuanced understanding of state violence and gender (in)equalities must consider the varied and contradictory experiences of armed civilian women, female soldiers, and opponents of gun possession. How are "feminism" and "femininity" negotiated in the early 21st century by civilian and military women in a nation that fetishizes guns? This book addresses this social problem by offering a comparative analysis of the particular dilemmas that gender inequality, class inequality, race/racism, and U.S. nationalism generate for women of diverse backgrounds who are struggling to balance conventional gender roles, femininity, and gendered violence in the United States.

France Winddance Twine is Professor of Sociology at the University of California, Santa Barbara. She is an ethnographer, a critical race theorist, and a documentary filmmaker who earned her degree at the University of California, Berkeley. She has published more than 60 books, journal articles, book reviews, and essays. She is the author and an editor of eight books, including *Geographies of Privilege* (forthcoming, 2013), *A White Side of Black Britain: Interracial Intimacy and Racial Literacy* (2010), *Outsourcing the Womb: Race, Class, and Gestational Surrogacy in a Global Market* (Routledge, 2011), *Retheorizing Race and Whiteness in the 21st Century* (with Charles Gallagher, Routledge, 2011), and *Feminism and Antiracism: International Struggles for Justice* (New York University Press, 2000). She has served as deputy editor of *American Sociological Review*, the official journal of the American Sociological Association. Twine currently serves on the international editorial boards of the journals *Ethnic and Racial Studies*; *Sociology*, the official journal of the British Sociological Association; and *Identities: Global Studies in Culture and Power*.

WI

University Readers
Reading Materials Evolved.

THE SOCIAL ISSUES
COLLECTION

Routledge
Taylor & Francis Group

Framing 21st Century Social Issues

The goal of this new, unique Series is to offer readable, teachable "thinking frames" on today's social problems and social issues by leading scholars. These are available for view on http://routledge.custom-gateway.com/routledge-social-issues.html.

For instructors teaching a wide range of courses in the social sciences, the Routledge *Social Issues Collection* now offers the best of both worlds: originally written short texts that provide "overviews" to important social issues *as well as* teachable excerpts from larger works previously published by Routledge and other presses.

As an instructor, click to the website to view the library and decide how to build your custom anthology and which thinking frames to assign. Students can choose to receive the assigned materials in print and/or electronic formats at an affordable price.

Available

Body Problems
Running and Living Long in a Fast-Food Society
Ben Agger

Sex, Drugs, and Death
Addressing Youth Problems
in American Society
Tammy Anderson

The Stupidity Epidemic
Worrying About Students, Schools,
and America's Future
Joel Best

Empire Versus Democracy
The Triumph of Corporate and Military Power
Carl Boggs

Contentious Identities
Ethnic, Religious, and Nationalist Conflicts
in Today's World
Daniel Chirot

The Future of Higher Education
Dan Clawson and Max Page

Waste and Consumption
Capitalism, the Environment, and
the Life of Things
Simonetta Falasca-Zamponi

Rapid Climate Change
Causes, Consequences, and Solutions
Scott G. McNall

The Problem of Emotions in Societies
Jonathan H. Turner

Outsourcing the Womb
Race, Class, and Gestational Surrogacy
in a Global Market
France Winddance Twine

Changing Times for Black Professionals
Adia Harvey Wingfield

Why Nations Go to War
A Sociology of Military Conflict
Mark P. Worrell

How Ethical Systems Change: Eugenics, the Final Solution, Bioethics
Sheldon Ekland-Olson and Julie Beicken

How Ethical Systems Change: Abortion and Neonatal Care
Sheldon Ekland-Olson and Elyshia Aseltine

How Ethical Systems Change: Tolerable Suffering and Assisted Dying
Sheldon Ekland-Olson and Elyshia Aseltine

How Ethical Systems Change: Lynching and Capital Punishment
Sheldon Ekland-Olson and Danielle Dirks

Nuclear Family Values, Extended Family Lives
The Power of Race, Class, and Gender
Natalia Sarkisian and Naomi Gerstel

Disposable Youth, Racialized Memories, and the Culture of Cruelty
Henry Giroux

Due Process Denied: Detentions and Deportations in the United States
Tanya Golash-Boza

Oversharing: Presentation of Self in the Internet Age
Ben Agger

Foreign Remedies: What the Experience of Other Nations Can Tell Us about Next Steps in Reforming U.S. Health Care
David A. Rochefort and Kevin P. Donnelly

DIY: The Search for Control and Self-Reliance in the 21st Century
Kevin Wehr

Torture
A Sociology of Violence and Human Rights
Lisa Hajjar

Terror
Social, Political, and Economic Perspectives
Mark Worrell

Girls with Guns
Firearms, Feminism, and Militarism
France Winddance Twine

Forthcoming

Are We Coddling Prisoners?
Benjamin Fleury-Steiner

Identity Problems in the Facebook Era
Daniel Trottier

Trafficking and Terror
Pardis Mahdavi

Beyond the Prison Industrial Complex
Kevin Weher and Elyshia Aseltine

Color Line?
Race and Sport in America
Krystal Beamon

Unequal Prospects
Is Working Longer the Answer?
Tay McNamara and John Williamson

iTime
Ben Agger

Girls with Guns
Firearms, Feminism, and Militarism

France Winddance Twine
University of California, Santa Barbara

Routledge
Taylor & Francis Group

NEW YORK AND LONDON

First published 2013
by Routledge
711 Third Avenue, New York, NY 10017

Simultaneously published in the UK
by Routledge
2 Park Square, Milton Park, Abingdon, Oxon OX14 4RN

Routledge is an imprint of the Taylor & Francis Group, an informa business

Library of Congress Cataloging in Publication Data

Twine, France Winddance
Girls with guns : firearms, feminism, and militarism / France Winddance Twine.
p. cm. — (Framing 21st century social issues)
Includes bibliographical references and index.
1. Firearms—Social aspects. 2. Violence in women. 3. Shooters of firearms.
4. Sex role. 5. Feminism. I. Title.
HQ1233.T95 2013
305.48'42—dc23   2012029134

ISBN: 978-0-415-51673-0 (pbk)
ISBN: 978-0-203-07113-7 (ebk)

Typeset in Adobe Garamond pro
by Cenveo Publisher Services

Printed and bound in the United States of America by Publishers Graphics,
LLC on sustainably sourced paper.

Contents

Series Foreword   ix

Preface   xi

Acknowledgments   xiii

I. The Woman's Gun Market   1

II. "Bad Girls" in a Gun Nation: Race, Citizenship, and Political Dissidents   12

III. The Mommy Wars: The National Debate on Gun Regulation   25

IV. Firearms Feminism and Militarized Femininity   36

V. The Economics of Military Motherhood   56

VI. Double Jeopardy: Female Soldiers in the Military–Sexual Complex   60

VII. Conclusion: Gender Equality in the U.S. Armed Forces   68

Bibliography   72

Glossary/Index   77

Series Foreword

The world in the early 21st century is beset with problems—a troubled economy, global warming, oil spills, religious and national conflict, poverty, HIV, health problems associated with sedentary lifestyles. Virtually no nation is exempt, and everyone, even in affluent countries, feels the impact of these global issues.

Since its inception in the 19th century, sociology has been the academic discipline dedicated to analyzing social problems. It is still so today. Sociologists offer not only diagnoses; they glimpse solutions, which they then offer to policy makers and citizens who work for a better world. Sociology played a major role in the civil rights movement during the 1960s in helping us to understand racial inequalities and prejudice, and it can play a major role today as we grapple with old and new issues.

This series builds on the giants of sociology, such as Weber, Durkheim, Marx, Parsons, and Mills. It uses their frames, and newer ones, to focus on particular issues of contemporary concern. These books are about the nuts and bolts of social problems, but they are equally about the frames through which we analyze these problems. It is clear by now that there is no single correct way to view the world, but only paradigms, models, which function as lenses through which we peer. For example, in analyzing oil spills and environmental pollution, we can use a frame that views such outcomes as unfortunate results of a reasonable effort to harvest fossil fuels. "Drill, baby, drill" sometimes involves certain costs as pipelines rupture and oil spews forth. Or we could analyze these environmental crises as inevitable outcomes of our effort to dominate nature in the interest of profit. The first frame would solve oil spills with better environmental protection measures and clean-ups, while the second frame would attempt to prevent them altogether, perhaps shifting away from the use of petroleum and natural gas and toward alternative energies that are "green."

These books introduce various frames such as these for viewing social problems. They also highlight debates between social scientists who frame problems differently. The books suggest solutions, both on the macro and micro levels. That is, they suggest what new policies might entail, and they also identify ways in which people, from the ground level, can work toward a better world, changing themselves and their lives and families and providing models of change for others.

Readers do not need an extensive background in academic sociology to benefit from these books. Each book is student-friendly in that we provide glossaries of terms for the uninitiated that are keyed to bolded terms in the text. Each chapter ends with questions for further thought and discussion. The level of each book is accessible to undergraduate students, even as these books offer sophisticated and innovative analyses.

This is the third year of our Routledge social issues book series. These brief books explore key contemporary social problems in ways that introduce basic concepts in the social sciences, cover key literature in the field, and offer original analyses and diagnoses. Our series includes books on topics ranging widely from global warming, to global ethnic conflict, to comparative healthcare, to oversharing on the Internet. These readable treatments can be assigned in both lower- and upper-division sociology courses in which instructors seek affordable, pithy treatments of social problems.

France Winddance Twine's book on guns is especially timely in light of recent mass shootings and subsequent debates over gun ownership and gun control. Her unique contribution is to examine women gun owners, from historical and contemporary perspectives.

Preface

How does the social, political, and economic status of a woman inform her relationship to guns and violence? How do civilian women differ from professional soldiers in their experiences with guns and gendered violence? What can we learn about femininity and feminism from women who arm themselves for the nation as professional soldiers? This book offers a comparative analysis of the experiences of female civilians (armed and unarmed) and female soldiers. This book raises questions about the complicated relationship between "feminism" and "femininity" from the perspective of armed women (both civilian and military). It draws on the experiences of U.S. women of diverse backgrounds in terms of their political ideology, race/ethnicity, marital status, and occupation. This includes women who are: 1) recreational gun owners (heritage hunters, competitive target shooters, casual shooters); 2) self-defenders; 3) women who do not own firearms; and 4) professional soldiers and members of the U.S. Armed Services.

A comparative analysis of civilian and military women offers important insights into how women negotiate their sexuality, femininity, and gender inequalities in a nation in which guns are fetishized and easily accessible. In the 1990s the United States witnessed a new wave of gun violence which led to national debates about the need for federal legislation that increased regulations and restrictions on gun sales and those opposed to more gun regulation.

These "gun wars" divided women, particularly mothers, into two camps. While the gun wars raged among the civilian population, more and more young women from working-class and impoverished families turned to the military as an institution that could provide stable employment.

The military is the single largest employer of youth in the United States today. In 2006 the U.S. Armed Forces, which includes the U.S. Army, Air Force, Marine Corps, Navy, and Coast Guard, enlisted almost 200,000 new recruits and employed nearly 700,000 men and women under the age of 25. As a result a significant number of women are first exposed to firearms and obtain weapons training as female soldiers and employees of the U.S. Armed Services. Regardless of whether they are in positions classified as "combat," women in the army undergo some weapons training.

Acknowledgments

I have been fortunate to have a talented and tenacious research assistant, Melissa MacDonald, who conducted several interviews for this book and graciously tracked down references. I thank Alicia Waldas, the founder of Safely in Mothers' Arms, for agreeing to be interviewed and for her permission to publish excerpts from the interview in this book. Paul Amar, Paola Bacchetta, Lisa Hajjar, Joseph Jewell, Melissa MacDonald, Joane Nagel, and Jan Neverdeen Pieterse, all helped me think through sections of this book and kept me smiling throughout the writing of this. I thank Esther Lezra, Debbie Rogow, and Howie Winant for always being there when I needed a break and for going to Shabbat services with me when I needed a spiritual boost. I thank Sergei Onishenko for keeping me physically fit and balanced by teaching me boxing and meditation. Rabbi Steve Cohen, Allan Cronin, Steve Twine, and my Chicago cousins inspired me to think about militarism and its impact on women and their families.

1: The Woman's Gun Market

In 1890 the frontier was officially "closed" by the U.S. government, thus ending an era of European-American conquest, genocide, and colonization that has been romanticized and sanitized. During this period, which coincided with the **Victorian era** (1860–1901), Wild West shows became a popular form of mass entertainment. In these shows, White women and men, along with dispossessed Native Americans, staged reenactments of the conquest of the frontier that featured the last remaining "wild" Indians and celebrated Anglo-American supremacy. Wild West shows also provided an opportunity for White women to display their target shooting skills while not formally challenging gender inequality or male supremacy.

Although target shooting was arguably one of the first sports where women competed equally with men, target shooting was not perceived as "feminist," that is as evidence of increasing gender equality, or as necessarily a disruption of conventional gender roles. On the Western frontier, where Native Americans were still being "removed" and were engaged in an ongoing war with the Anglo-Americans who wanted their land, White women were given weapons, and taught how to use them properly to protect themselves and their homes.

During the Victorian era, firearms in the hands of young girls (children) and young women were perceived and represented in advertisements as a natural and appropriate leisure activity for White girls and women of all ages. The vast majority of the population lived in rural areas where guns were not perceived as dangerous weapons (unless in the hands of slaves, Blacks, or Native Americans) but rather as recreational toys and necessary tools in everyday life on the frontier.

Annie Oakley was born Phoebe Ann Moses in 1860. A Midwesterner from Ohio, she became a celebrity target shooter in 1887 while performing in Buffalo Bill Cody's Wild West Show. Three decades before women in the United States would be granted suffrage, the right to vote as full citizens, Annie Oakley, a proper married lady, embraced traditional gender roles and opposed women's **suffrage**. Although there were other very skilled women target shooters of "racially ambiguous" origins Oakley was regarded as the best White female target shooter of that period. Whiteness along with a gendered performance that was recognized as upper-middle class was essential to Annie Oakley's popularity. In other words she was an anti-feminist.

In an analysis of why Annie Oakley became so popular in comparison with some of the other target shooters who may have been equally skilled such as Lillian Smith, a young White woman, who became famous after joining Buffalo Bill's Wild West

Show, Browder argues that Oakley's popularity rested on the fact that she emphasized her White femininity, her girlishness, and thus did not challenge gender inequalities. Instead, she upheld them by presenting herself as a non-threatening anti-feminist opposed to women's suffrage. In Browder's words, "What distinguished Annie Oakley was that she presented herself as a Victorian lady who also happened to be an expert markswoman" (2006: 86). In other words, Oakley carefully cultivated a particular form of Victorian femininity while on stage by not wearing pants (as did female outlaws) and behaving as a "lady." This distinguished her both racially and culturally from her contemporaries who were working for competing shows.

Instead of redefining or expanding the boundaries of femininity for respectable women, Oakley embraced very conventional gender norms off-stage and on-stage by strategically employing Victorian femininity to earn a living as a target shooter. She did this, in part, by her style of dress and by distancing herself from what were called "bloomer women" (feminists and other women who wore pants) and refusing to support women's struggle for the right to vote. In the words of Laura Browder:

> Oakley neither smoked, drank, gambled, nor cursed…. She was outraged when people saw her as a "new woman." Her act was clean cut and wholesome; she often included her manager-husband, to whom she remained married for the rest of her life, and their dog in performances. Oakley was instrumental not only in attracting women to the Wild West show but also in making shooting appear something that even a lady could comfortably do. Oakley's trademark skip and pout, her use of her dog and her husband in her act, and even her childlessness helped her present herself as a dutiful daughter with a spunky side.
>
> (2006: 89)

Advertisements for firearms produced during the Victorian era, which coincided with the first wave of the feminist movement, depicted middle-class White women using guns as part of their recreation. These ads differed radically from those produced in the latter half of the 20th century after World War II. In *Her Best Shot: Women and Guns in America*, the historian Laura Browder found that:

> [T]he early ads featuring women and guns showed guns to be safe tools to be used as equipment for healthy recreation …. Outdoor recreation … was considered by political and social leaders to be key to building a racially strong nation filled with vigorous, fertile white women. By contrast, weapon ads since the 1980s have encouraged women to buy guns not as part of an explicit nation-building effort but as a defense against anonymous violence, a task that the government is clearly not up to.
>
> (2006: 9–10)

Despite the fact that guns were symbols of masculinity, women and even young girls of European and Anglo-American ancestry have always had access to guns. However, access to small arms and the use of guns have varied across time and region. During the period of nation-building when Europeans were still colonizing what was then called "Indian Territory" and would later be land given to White "homesteaders," guns were perceived and treated as household tools that White women and men on the frontier needed. We also learn from Browder that young girls appeared armed in gun advertisements:

> Guns were presented as so unthreatening that they were safe for young girls, as well as for women. An 1891 calendar for the Union Metallic Cartridge Company shows a girl, who cannot be more than four or five years old, surrounded by eight hunting dogs and carrying a rifle.
>
> (2006: 5)

An analysis of the popularity of female target shooters such as Annie Oakley and her competitors reveal that armed women were celebrated and accepted as "entertainers" during an era of state-sanctioned male supremacy. During this period women were denied the right to vote, own property in their own name in most states, and could not enter into legal contracts. Moreover, the advertisements from the Victorian era are a reminder that a cultural analysis of armed girls and armed women must be firmly situated in the historical context. Victorian pro-gun ideologies contrast sharply with today's representation of guns as dangerous and harmful to children by proponents of increased federal gun regulation.

Modern-Day Gun Women

Chicks with Guns is a glossy photography book that presents brief cultural portraits of 78 women gun owners from across the United States. Lindsay McCrum, the photographer and author of *Chicks with Guns*, argues that she is providing a "politically neutral" book. This beautiful photographic book presents a very selective portrait of women of diverse ages (mainly White) who own, collect, love, and use their guns in competitive shooting, law enforcement, and self-defense. More than half of the portraits are women from three states—Texas, California, and Montana.

On the cover of *Chick with Guns*, is a stunning photograph of Greta, a young White girl from Napa Valley (a wine region in northern California), who played Annie Oakley on public television. Greta is photographed with an 1820 English Forsyth-system scent-bottle pistol. On the wall above her hang four long-barrel rifles. Greta describes how she developed a relationship with guns:

> I was only seven or eight months old when I received my first gun, a gift from a longtime friend of my parents. A miniature stocked Colt 1861 navy revolver.

It has a personalized inscription with an engraved stock…. In 2006, I played the young Annie Oakley in a PBS American Experience production. Originally I was only supposed to be in a short outdoor clip, but after the producer saw the footage of me shooting flyers with a 20 gauge double barrel shotgun, she also wanted me to portray Annie Oakley on stage. If you watch the footage, you will see me shooting a Frank Wesson single shot .22 target rifle as well as a Stevens .22 single shot target pistol, which are the same types of guns Annie Oakley used in her performances.

(McCrum 2011: 30–31)

More than 125 years after Annie Oakley mesmerized Americans with her shooting skills, competitive target shooting remains a popular sport across rural and urban America. In 2008 Sarah Palin was selected to be the Republican vice-presidential candidate. Palin, a former beauty contestant and then the 44-year-old mother of five children, quickly became a modern-day Annie Oakley—although with political ambitions that Oakley, an opponent of women's suffrage, lacked. As a political candidate she utilized her relationship to guns, particularly hunting big game, as a way to appeal to her constituency. She did this in a way that enhanced, rather than diminished, her femininity. By hunting with her manicured nails and charismatic smile, whether intentional or not, Palin resurrected and recycled an image of the armed White Victorian mother engaged in healthy recreational shooting.

In a 2008 article the *Sun*, a British tabloid, described Sarah Palin's relationship to guns:

Sarah Palin learned to shoot at an early age. She got to grips with a gun at eight and made her first kill at ten. The moose-hunting mum of five from Alaska grew up shooting animals and skinning them on the spot before hauling the meat home to the family freezer.

(Smith 2008: 8)

As a Republican candidate and a member of the National Rifle Association (NRA), Palin repeatedly described and promoted herself to conservative voters as a skilled hunter, a rifle owner, and a target shooter. She marketed herself to her Republican constituents as an "average" American mother and gun owner. Her affection for guns and hunting appealed to White male conservative voters and to the radical right wing of the Republican Party. As an attractive woman and an avid hunter, Palin embraced a form of leisure that is associated with masculinity in the United States. Palin marketed herself as a civilian, a wife, and a mother, who enjoyed using lethal weapons to kill animals for sport. In what has been called a "gunfighter" nation, this is a significant form of cultural capital among some voting constituencies in parts of the United States.

On November 14, 2010 The Learning Channel (TLC) began airing an eight-part travelogue miniseries called *Sarah Palin's Alaska*. Mark Burnett, the producer of this series was also the producer of *Survivor*, one of the highest-rated TV reality shows. The first episode of this miniseries attracted an estimated audience of five million people, breaking all previous records for viewership. After being approved for a second season, the show was canceled in the aftermath of Palin's controversial remarks in response to the shooting of Congresswoman Gabrielle Giffords. The show received mixed reviews from critics who found it disappointing.

In a review of the series, Nick Jans argues that Palin's ability to handle a rifle demonstrated that the gun girl whom Sarah Palin had marketed herself as more closely resembled a "fictional character" and that she failed to demonstrate the level of competence with a hunting rifle that one would expect from someone who had grown up hunting. In his words:

> Those of us who have actually lived off the land are less than impressed by Palin's televised exploits and, more important, by what they tell us about her. Tentative, physically inept, and betraying an even more awkward unfamiliarity with the land and lifestyle that's supposedly her birthright, Palin deconstructs her own myth before our eyes.
>
> (Jans 2011)

In the case of Sarah Palin, her love of guns and supposed facility with them was central to her orchestrated presentation of herself as an authentic American as opposed to the university-educated and unarmed Americans she regularly mocks. With perfectly manicured French nails, Palin does not carry her gun, or load her own gun. Rather her father loads it for her. Her less than stellar performance as a markswoman suggests that she may have exaggerated her shooting skills—using them as a form of political currency among the conservative NRA element of the Republican Party. In what Jans calls "orchestrated reality," we see that Palin is less of a skilled gun girl and more of a skilled political performer. Registering disappointment, Jans critiques her performance:

> [H]er father repeatedly works the bolt and loads for her as she misses shots after shot before scoring a kill on the seventh round—enough bullets for a decent hunter to take down at least five animals…. Later Palin blames the scope, but any marksman would recognize the flinching, the unsteady aim and poor shot selection— and the glaring ethical fault of both shooter and gun owner if the rifle wasn't properly sighted.
>
> (Jans 2011)

Palin's relationship to guns has been central to her media image and her national celebrity. The success of her television series suggests that representations of a White mother who arms herself on the weekends to go hunting is an appealing and powerful symbol that resonates with Tea Party activists and the extreme right wing of the Republican Party. Like Annie Oakley and the representations of armed Victorian women in popular advertisements, rather than being diminished, Palin's femininity was enhanced by her participation in a sport associated with masculinity. As an iconic White gun girl, Palin's popularity among conservative voters demonstrates the political allure of armed White women who carefully represent themselves as conventionally feminine.

Scholars who have analyzed the relationship between gun ownership, gun rights, Whiteness, and citizenship have shown how gun ownership and citizenship have been intertwined with gender inequalities in the United States. While racial and ethnic minorities historically were denied the right to possess guns, during specific historical moments, White women have been encouraged to take up arms in the defense of White nation-building projects.

The Gender Gap in Gun Ownership

How many women personally own a gun? According to a Gallup poll of 1,012 American adults conducted between October 13–16 in 2005, there is a **gender gap** in gun ownership, with only 13 percent of American women reporting owning a gun. The reasons that women reported owning a gun did not differ from those of men. They were motivated by: 1) fear of crime; 2) target shooting; and 3) hunting. Statistics on gun ownership that rely on self-report are not completely reliable. There may be much higher rates of gun ownership among women than appear in polling data.

> Not only is it impossible to ascertain the precise number of women who own or have access to or regularly use firearms, the extensive social-scientific literature on guns and their use almost invariably fails to take gender into account. Thus, most of the conclusions extrapolated from that literature arise from and support a masculinist perspective on guns and gun use—since conventionally, most gun owners and users have been males, as have most victims of gun-related violence. How we wondered, might the numbers look different if we recognized that a small, but nevertheless significant, proportion of guns are in women's hands? How might the debate about guns and gun control change if female gun owners were taken into account?
>
> (Stange and Oyster 2000: 7)

A 2005 Gallup poll reported that three in ten Americans personally own a gun; most gun owners say that they use guns to protect themselves against crime, for hunting, and for target shooting. This poll found that the majority of Americans do not own guns with 57 percent reporting that they did not own a gun. The 2005 Gallup poll found "essentially no change since the questions were last asked in 2000. At that time, 27% of American said they personally owned a gun, another 14% said another household member owned one". This poll also found that gun ownership varies according to race, gender, region, and political affiliation. Men are more likely than women to personally own a gun. Republicans are more likely than Democrats, and White men, particularly residents of the Midwest and South, own guns at a rate much higher than men who reside in other regions of the United States.

Polls are not completely reliable sources of data and we must therefore take into account the biases and exclusions in any polling data. What we don't learn from the Gallup poll is how the civilian gun-owning population differs from those female gun owners who are or have been employed by the police forces or the U.S. Armed Services. Military women are invisible in the analyses offered in these statistics. What can we learn from a comparative analysis of armed civilian women and female soldiers employed by the Armed Forces?

According to a 2011 Gallup poll survey on crime, there has been a significant shift in every demographic and attitudinal group towards a pro-gun stance. In 1990 78 percent of Americans polled wanted stricter gun control laws when surveyed by Gallup. In 2009, it had dropped significantly with only 44 percent of Americans surveyed reported wanting stricter laws regulating the sale of firearms (Jones 2009). Now Gallup polls must be interpreted with caution in the context of a society that fetishizes guns.

Until 2011 the annual Gallup Crime Poll had always found a significantly higher percentage of Americans advocating stricter gun laws. This poll showed a new low in the percentage of Americans favoring a ban on handgun possession except by the police and other authorized person, a question that dates back to 1959. Only 28 percent now favor such a ban. The high point in support for a handgun-possession ban was 60 percent in the initial measurement in 1959.

In addition to increased support of handgun ownership, there were two other major findings in the 2011 poll. There were no reported major changes in personal gun ownership; in other words, there was no increase in ownership among those polled and the racial and gender gap remains with *White men being the largest demographic reporting gun ownership*. However, this poll also reflected a class gap in which higher levels of education were associated with those who favor stricter gun laws.

The Lady Smith Handgun and the Women's Gun Market

In 1857 Smith & Wesson, a small arms manufacturer in Springfield, Massachusetts, began selling the first commercially available revolver to chamber metallic cartridge. Smith & Wesson became a leading supplier of handguns of all types for the next

154 years. This company has become a primary supplier of handguns to police, the military, and to the civilian marketplace. Small-frame revolvers were available as early as the 1950s and by 1998 Smith & Wesson had expanded its product line to include their revolver models and 32 pistol models, many with two or more variations.

Although guns had been advertised and available to women for hundreds of years, the deployment of feminist rhetoric to market guns to women as a 'niche' market did not occur before 1989. There are some notable changes that are worth considering that distinguish gun sales to women in prior generations.

The year 1989 was a watershed year for the gun industry and its relationship to women as consumers for a number of reasons. First, in March of 1989 Smith & Wesson, the leading manufacturer of handguns, introduced a new line of handguns designed for women called the Lady Smith handgun. These handguns were marketed as "feminine" revolvers and ranged in price from $399 to $450. Constructed with rosewood handles and small grips, a svelte .38 caliber revolver was scaled down and rounded to better fit a woman's hands. The Lady Smith guns were designed for handbags and feminine shoulder-holsters. While they were not the first small handguns, they were more fashionable than earlier models that had been available.

How did Smith & Wesson repackage and redefine guns as "feminine" in a national culture in which guns remain an icon of masculinity and violence? Smith & Wesson redesigned their product line to sell to people outside of their core market of White males by developing and launching an advertising campaign that hijacked the language of **feminism** and female empowerment. In their "Refuse to Be a Victim" campaign they strategically deployed the rhetoric of empowerment to encourage women to empower themselves by purchasing the latest designer handguns. Glossy ads were placed in women's magazines such as *The Ladies Home Journal*, which depicted White mothers tucking their children in bed and a revolver on the nightstand. Opponents of the NRA argued that they appropriated feminist language of "empowerment," employed fear, and targeted White mothers in their ads to promote guns sales. In 1990 the NRA created a women's issues division.

The handgun market can be divided into five segments: 1) recreational; 2) competition; 3) hunting; 4) self-defense; and 5) police/military. Why did small arms manufacturers like Smith & Wesson begin targeting women as a niche market? Handgun sales sharply declined and this became evident by 1995. By 1996 sales had fallen to a little over half of their 1994 peak. There was increased competition from Taurus Marketing, a Brazilian manufacturer that produced a high-quality gun resembling the Smith & Wesson, for 30–35 percent below the U.S. market price. Taurus, a major player in the light arms market, directly competed with Smith & Wesson.

In a sociological study of the national survey data, Joseph Shely, Charles Brody, and James Wright challenged the demographic portraits presented in the mainstream press and concluded that between 1973 and 1991 there were no changes in gun ownership. They argued that:

> [T]he proportion of women—and men—owning guns was effectively constant … women's gun ownership is no more closely related to fear of crime or experiences with crime than is men's, and, for women, the relation between fear of crime and gun ownership has not changed in recent years. In short, the female gun owner has not come to approximate the portraiture of the upscale, affluent, single "women about town" as depicted in the popular literature.
>
> (1994: 219)

Media portrayals of gun ownership among (presumably White) women, they argued, were inflated by the gun industry and not based on national survey data. The gun industry has provided data that suggests that there has been a dramatic increase in the number of women gun owners. The mainstream media reporting on women and gun ownership reflects an uncritical acceptance of sales figures that have been provided by the gun industry (Herbert 1994). In *Blown Away*, Caitlin Kelly also cites studies that suggest that media campaigns to sell guns may not be radically transforming the gun-owning demographic.

> A 1995 study of 396 men and women found that "women's attitudes towards guns and the ownership of them do not seem to be influenced by marketing campaigns directed at them, but instead seem to be complex reflections of societal and personal influences." In other words, women choose guns for more complicated reasons than simply seeing an advertisement or hearing a fear-mongering slogan.
>
> (Kelly 2004: 92)

In a comparative analysis of gun advertisements in the 1890s and gun magazines in the 1990s, Browder discovers a key difference in their goals. She reminds the reader that gun magazines that targeted women in the 1990s

> avoided using titillating or violent images of the armed woman. Yet there is a crucial difference between the purpose of gun advertising and the goal of the new magazine…. To prosper, these magazines … must do more than sell firearms products, they must create an imagined community of armed women, in a way that can reach as many women as possible.
>
> (2006: 214)

The questions remain: "Who belongs to this 'imagined' community of women gun owners?" and "What distinguishes women who purchase guns for leisure, recreation, and target shooting from female soldiers and from armed civilians who purchase guns primarily to defend themselves against violence?"

Guns are polysemic. They have multiple and competing meanings depending upon the context in which they are used (social, historical, professional, leisure, national). In the United States, a nation that was formed out of genocide, slavery, and industrialization, specific national narratives have been constructed to resolve the contradictions between routinized violence and democracy. The meaning of gun ownership and gun use has been shaped by U.S. nationalism and the narratives that we have inherited. In *Mortal Stakes*, Jan Dizard argues that:

> By the early twentieth century, hunting was thoroughly folded into a national narrative that celebrated the taming of the continent and the dawning of an age when engagements with nature could be structured by a sporting ethic which borrowed elements from elite traditions but which was thoroughly bourgeois: the emphasis was on self-restraint, regard for property, refinement of technique, and the embrace of objective natural history.
>
> (2003: 41)

There are many routes to gun ownership and gun use in the United States. There are women who, like Sarah Palin, are "**heritage hunters**"; as children, they inherited gun training and the experience of hunting was something passed down from their parents and family members. For this group, hunting is routine, ritualized, and often done communally. A second group of female gun owners, which I refer to as the "defenders," are motivated primarily by fears and concerns with safety, self-defense, and protection. They may have witnessed or survived an assault, robbery, or some other violent crime or they may live alone in areas that they perceive as dangerous.

Competitive target shooters, a third category of women, use guns as a pleasurable leisure activity to acquire valued shooting skills. Their primary goal is not to use lethal force to kill but to display their target-shooting abilities. A fourth category of women gun users are the "professionals"; this includes women employed as soldiers or armed professionals including police officers, security personnel or in related occupations that authorize them to use lethal weapons.

DISCUSSION QUESTIONS

1. Do an internet search and select two gun *magazines* or *websites* that target female consumers and/or gun owners. Based upon your analysis of the feature articles, advertisements, and visual images, describe in detail the type of women being targeted by these magazines/websites as an ideal gun owner/reader (age, occupation, educational level, race/ethnicity, class background, region). In other words who is the imagined community of gun owners for these magazines?

2. Look for images of armed women in the popular media (films, cable television, internet, and print magazines). What is their age, race, ethnicity, presumed class, maternal status? What is their motivation for using guns? What types of gun are they shown carrying? In the case of advertisements, what types of product (other than guns) are being marketed?

3. Go online and search for firearms and gun-related products that target women consumers. What types of women are visually depicted in their ads? Describe them based on their presumed age, marital status, maternal status, race? What type of woman appears to be the targeted consumer based on the photographs and visual representations? Is she married? Is she single? Is she a mother? Is she White?

4. Given the high degree of gendered violence (particularly rape and sexual assault) in the United States, how can girls and young women be trained in the use of lethal weapons to defend themselves? Is weapons training for women and teenage girls a reasonable response (and potential solution) to the problem of gun violence, a crime in which men are overrepresented as perpetrators?

II: "Bad Girls" in a Gun Nation

Race, Citizenship, and Political Dissidents

Gun Molls and the Gender Outlaws of the 1930s

During the mid-1930s the Federal Department of Investigation began to identify, arrest, and prosecute White women for federal crimes connected to gang-related activity. The White women who were prosecuted were known as **gun molls**. Gun molls were the romantic, sexual, and, in some cases, bank-robbing partners of men engaged in criminal activities that included kidnapping, contract murders, protection rackets, and gun running. As White women of rural origin and from working-class backgrounds, like the celebrity target shooters, they were not from economically privileged backgrounds and had work histories. They had moved to urban areas like Chicago to work which brought them into social contact with men involved in organized crime. One of the most famous gun molls was Bonnie Parker, a member of the Bonnie and Clyde gang.

These women were often minor celebrities in their own right, but most often they functioned as the "wives," girlfriends, and companions of men engaged in violent crime. Although they violated some heterosexual gender conventions by using and carrying weapons, they also conformed to some gender norms. Most gun molls did not use arms as mothers protecting their children and families, but as armed criminals. Drawing upon the life histories of 20 women in the Dillinger gang, the scholar Claire Potter concludes that molls were characterized in the following way:

> A moll was relatively young: most frequently, she was also native-born, of European descent, and the child of farming parents or skilled workers…. These women stuck it out alone: none of them were living with their parents when they were introduced to bandit life. We should also note that none of these women worked in factories, despite the fact that industrial laborers were paid better, had regular hours, and were subject to less sexual harassment from male supervisors. Instead future molls worked in nightclubs, retail, and food service: jobs where they would meet men—and men with money to spend.
>
> (1995: 47)

Prior to the 1930s White women who were involved in organized crime were relatively invisible in the national press and were not targeted by federal authorities.

This changed in 1934 when J. Edgar Hoover initiated a campaign to target and arrest women who were linked to criminals. Gun molls became the targets of federal investigation, and popular folk heroes and celebrity outlaws. In distinguishing gun molls from prostitutes, Potter defines the complex and contradictory status of the gangster girls of the 1930s:

> Previous to the twentieth century the moll was either an independent sex worker or a resident of a disorderly house. More important, a moll, or "molly," was not necessarily a woman: "she" was often male, a man masquerading as a woman and/or someone of another class. Add to this heady sexuality, undefinable except by what it is not (heterosexually male), the phallic power which a gun invokes and the gun moll becomes a location where desire and danger, female and male, familiar and transgressive sexualities intersect.
>
> (1995: 44)

Although guns had always been available to White women, among urban women and particularly unmarried women gun use was primarily not for "professional" reasons, since women were not employed by law enforcement in significant numbers at this time. The gangster girls of the 1930s used guns to survive economically and to support their "families." The armed civilians of the early 20th century share an economic background with many 21st century female soldiers—one that provides few routes to upward mobility. They made decisions that, in their view, would bring them economic security and social mobility. A second characteristic of their life that bears some consideration is that, like female professional soldiers employed in the U.S. Armed Services and women employed as police officers, the gun women of the 1930s operated in a masculine world, one dominated by men and with a code of honor that required them to remain silent about the domestic violence and abuses they endured. We will see in later chapters that this has also been true of female soldiers, many of whom have witnessed and endured sexual abuse and other forms of violence within their military "families."

How did gun molls negotiate their femininity, and other gendered vulnerabilities (abortion, unwed pregnancy, domestic violence), in a male-dominated occupational and cultural environment organized around lethal violence? As gangster girls they often witnessed and participated in violence. According to Potter, one strategy employed by gun molls to normalize their relationships and represent themselves as conventional was to use the metaphor of traditional marriage.

> Female bandits created households and relationships with their bandit lovers which drew on the language and structures of conventional marriage. However, few of these women were actually married to the men they traveled with; many gang members, female and male, were married to other people altogether.... Gun molls

"spoke" to other women in a common language which depended on a fixed set of cultural assumptions, while it also disrupted them. They imagined a new realm of home and family in an outlaw world that emphasized female honor rather than social obligation, romance rather than domestic security.

(1995: 43–44)

Three decades after targeting the women known as "gun molls," J. Edgar Hoover would have to deal with a new group of women who were making extraordinary choices to live outside of the law, but these choices were not being made by uneducated women from rural areas with few career options. The gun women of the late 1960s and 1970s were often university-educated visionary feminist activists on the left. They regarded themselves as revolutionary political dissidents, who intended to transform the United States into a more egalitarian, humane, and democratic nation.

White Nationalism and Gun Ownership

The legal (authorized) possession of a gun has historically been a racialized and gendered privilege—a right of citizenship reserved for White men and later extended to White women for most of U.S. history. Adam Winkler, a professor of law at University of California, Los Angeles (UCLA) and a constitutional law scholar, summarizes the racialized gun restriction laws of the revolutionary era in what later became the United States.

> In the Revolutionary Era, gun laws were strict. Because there was no standing army the national defense depended upon an armed citizenry capable of fighting off invading European powers or hostile Native tribes. With national defense becoming too important to leave to individual choice or the free market, the founders implemented laws that required all **free men** between the ages of eight and forty-five to outfit themselves with a musket rifle or other firearm suitable for military service…. This mandate was enforced at musters public fathers held several times a year where every person eligible for militia service was required to attend, military gun in hand.
>
> (2011: 113; bold added; see glossary)

Legislation passed shortly after independence from Britain demonstrates the strong links established between Whiteness, maleness, and gun ownership. The earliest legislation prohibited anyone who as not socially classified as White and male from carrying weapons.

Laws dating back to the seventeenth century, such as the 1648 Virginia Law called An Act Preventing Negroes from Bearing Arms, limited the ability of non-whites to own guns. The **Uniform Militia Act of 1792** required free, able-bodied, white males between the ages of eighteen and forty-five to enroll in a militia, bearing their own arms and equipment, but it banned from service all slaves, freed blacks and Indians…. The politics of white supremacy in the South, both before and after the Civil War, mandated that whites use guns as instruments of terror to control blacks and that blacks be forbidden from using firearms.

(Browder 2006: 58; bold added; see glossary)

In his analysis of the historical debate over gun rights and gun regulation, Winkler reminds us that controlling gun ownership was central to the maintenance of White supremacy and control over slaves in the United States prior to abolition. He writes that White people were "[w]orried that slaves and free blacks would rise up and start a race war, many white southerners were terrified at the prospect of black men with guns" (2011: 132). Guns were used to socially and politically control the Black population whose civil rights had not yet been granted:

In the South, militias were transformed into slave patrols. Posses of armed whites would hunt down escaped slaves and terrorize free blacks. Laws, like the one enacted in Florida in 1825, specifically authorized patrols to "enter into all negro houses" and to "lawfully seize and take away" any "arms, weapons, and ammunition." As blacks were being further disarmed, the constitutional right to have guns was, ironically, expanding in other ways. Between 1790 and 1860, twenty states joined the Union, and fourteen of them included in their state constitutions the right to bear arms. In this period, the traditional militia justification for the right to bear arms was increasingly replaced by the notion that the right was primarily about personal defense against criminal attack.

(Winkler 2011: 133)

In the late 1960s in California, residents had the legal right to carry a weapon in public. A license was only required for a "concealed weapon." Thus, understanding the law, the Black Panther leadership understood that the police could not take away their right to openly carry and display a weapon in public if they were not threatening anyone. As residents of the State of California, they could openly carry weapons for their self-defense. They used their display of weapons to educate the Black public and the police.

Discussions of the importance of the "right to bear arms" in the United States suffer from historical amnesia in which authors tend to neglect, minimize, or fail to consider the racialized dimensions of gun ownership and the centrality of slavery and White nationalism to the sense of entitlement that some segments of the U.S. White population have regarding arms.

Women in the Black Panther Party for Self Defense

After leaving her day office job at UCLA, Elaine Brown would go to her night job working on the *Black Congress*, a newspaper published by the Black Panther Party. In 1974 when Huey Newton's self-exile to Cuba created a power vacuum in the organization, Brown became the first female leader of the Black Panther Party. In her memoir *A Taste of Power*, Brown describes her introduction to guns as a female member of the Black Panther Party:

> I did not resist when Crook strapped the two bandoliers of shotgun shells around my waist before taking me to the San Diego rally.... Guns were the natural accessory of the new black militants, who were determined to claim their manhood "by any means necessary."
>
> (1992: 128)

The **Black Panther Party for Self Defense** of Oakland was founded by Huey Newton and Bobby Seale, two college classmates in Oakland in 1966. Newton and Seale, both products of the Black migration from the South, founded an organization whose initial emphasis was upon defending the Black community from systematic police abuse, harassment, and state-sanctioned racism. The role of the Black Panthers, their political legacy, the treatment of women, struggles over gender equality in the organization, and the legacy of the Black Panther Party have been debated by many scholars. Here I want to focus on one issue on which there is no disagreement by scholars. *All members of the Black Panther Party, male and female, were trained in how to effectively use weapons. In this area, there were no gendered barriers.* The Black Panthers strategically employed guns as organizing tools, weapons for self-defense, and symbols of citizenship. They also provided some of the first media images of armed Black women who were trained like their male peers to effectively clean, load, and use weapons.

During the late 1960s the ownership and display of guns in the State of California was legal. The leaders of the Black Panthers studied the law and clearly understood their legal rights and their citizenship rights as Blacks, rights that Black people had not been allowed to exercise in other regions of the United States. JoNina M. Abron summarized California law at the time the Black Panthers began operating police patrols to defend their community.

In 1966, California statute permitted an individual to carry a loaded gun in public as long as it was not concealed and did not have a bullet in the chamber. Huey, Bobby, and other Panthers—armed with loaded weapons, cameras, law books, and tape recorders monitored the police in the Black community of Oakland. These Panther community patrols prevented incidents of police harassment and advised detained suspects of their legal rights. An avid student of the law, Huey gained a reputation for facing down police officers with a loaded shotgun, and for his mastery of the law.

(1998: 180)

Historians have given less attention to the roles of armed women in the Black Panther Party. With the exception of memoirs by former members such as Elaine Brown's *A Taste of Power*, there remains much to learn about the experiences of armed female members of the Black Panther Party. In a nation that has deprived Black men and women of the right to bear arms for much of its history, the images of armed Black women do not carry the same meaning (for non-Blacks) as those of armed White women. In the analysis of Linda Lumsden:

While fewer iconic images of African American women with guns exist—and virtually no widely disseminated images before the late 1960s—they carry a different charge for viewers schooled in the **semiotics** of the armed woman; these images generally suggest insurrection rather than criminality. Until the late nineteenth century, American guns laws, especially in the South, used racial ideology to limit ownership of firearms.... Given the long history of racialized gun laws, it is not surprising that the Black Panthers, most notably, claimed gun ownership for African Americans as a necessary element of American identity.

(2009: 14; bold added; see glossary)

Black women received the same training in weapons as their male peers:

Tarika Lewis (also known as Joan Lewis or Matilaba) is generally recognized as the first woman to officially join the Black Panther Party. A native of Oakland, California, Lewis attended Oakland Tech High School where she co-founded the Black Student Union, which staged sit-ins for Black Studies courses.... Lewis did not receive special treatment because she was a female. She explained that all organizational rules applying to the male members were also applicable to her. Lewis regularly attended political education classes and learned to disassemble, reassemble, clean and use firearms.

(LeBlanc-Ernest 1998: 307)

In his analysis of the goals and strategies of the Black Panther Party, Nikhil Pal Singh, a historian at New York University, explains why guns were central to the Panthers' political program in which they were "engaged in a war of conscience aimed at the transfiguration of a historical system of Black shame into one of pride and empowerment" (Singh 1998: 75). Singh argues that:

> The Panther's trademark actions of picking up the gun and patrolling the police ... were actually strategic choices and carefully posed challenges to the so-called legitimate forms of state violence that had become all too regularly used within Black communities.... Newton and Seale understood how the police had become the principal agents of official, state-sanctioned racism that had largely receded from public view only to be brutally reasserted.... By arming themselves with guns and law books and observing police behavior, the Panthers actually enacted a profound transvaluation of conventional racist imagery by exposing the most visible representatives of the law and the crucial transmission belt of state power as symbols of uniformed and armed lawlessness.
>
> (1998: 81)

In addition to community police patrols, Free Breakfast Programs, Free Rides to Prison Programs and other "survival programs," the Black Panthers published a newspaper which provided some of the first Black-produced images of armed Black women who were not pornographic objects, but rather political activists.

In an analysis of the Black Panther Party newspapers and their representations of Black women, Linda Lumsden concluded that "The Panther's most radical framing was illustrations of mothers with guns." Lumsden argues that:

> [The Black Panther Party] never portrayed Black women as sex objects or as consumers. The newspapers' verbal and visual rhetoric offered a paradoxical blend of traditional and radical frames of womanhood. Its most provocative imagery of mothers with guns fused militant Panther rhetoric advocating armed self-defense with the traditional image of woman as guardian of the home.
>
> (2009: 901)

The **Students for a Democratic Society (SDS)** was founded in 1960. Bernardine Dohrn, a 25-year-old native of Chicago and assistant executive secretary of the National Lawyers Guild, was elected to serve as the national leader of this organization. She would later end up on the Federal Bureau of Investigation's (FBI's) Most Wanted List. During the summer of 1968 the membership of the SDS peaked at an estimated 100,000 students.

Their task was clear—to organize thousands of youth to come to Chicago and demonstrate against the War in Vietnam, in support of the Black Panther Party, and in solidarity with political prisoners, including Black Panther, Huey P. Newton and the eight under attack for last summer's righteous demonstrations during the Democratic Party Convention.

(Jacobs 1997: 39)

On June 18, 1968 the SDS held their national convention in the Chicago Coliseum. At this conference the Chicago police behaved with such brutality and aggression that they became an international symbol of abusive state violence against unarmed student protestors. This marked a turning point in the New Left with some members shifting to the view that if state violence was going to be used against them, they would have to respond with violence. Describing the actions of the police, Dan Berger writes "The Chicago Police, at the direction of Mayor Richard Daley, went on a rampage against the demonstrators, refusing protest permits and revoking those granted—preferring instead some good, old-fashioned beatings. The cops waded through the crowds chanting 'kill, kill, kill'" (Berger 2006: 26).

The **Counter Intelligence Program** operated by the FBI beginning in the 1950s (and operated for several decades), known by the acronym Cointelpro, was a covert operation that employed and incited extralegal violence among and against members of civil rights organizations, anti-war student groups, revolutionary political groups, and social justice groups. The majority of the resources were *not* used to target hate groups or White supremacist organizations like the Ku Klux Klan but, instead, were directed against mainstream civil rights groups. Cointelpro was designed to discredit, disrupt, infiltrate, spy on, and harass members of progressive political groups. It is within this context that female members of organizations like the **Weatherman** began to perceive violence as an acceptable political strategy.

The Weatherman, an offshoot of the SDS, was founded in 1969 and is one of the most controversial and well-known of the New Left political groups. The name of the group was taken from a lyric "You don't need a weatherman to know which way the wind blows" in a 1963 Bob Dylan song called "Subterranean Homesick Blues." A paper, co-authored by Bernardine Dohrn, published in *New Left Notes* was titled "You Don't Need a Weatherman to Know Which Way the Wind Blows," and became the founding statement of the organization. This statement marked a transition from talking about political violence to engaging in armed insurrection and "It placed the struggle of black people in the United States at the forefront of the fight against US imperialism" (Jacobs 1997: 27).

In a political history of the Weather Underground, Ron Jacobs writes that the "Weatherman's analysis was virtually identical to that of the Panthers, especially in its insistence on black American's history of economic oppression" (Jacobs 1997:26).

The Black community was conceptualized as an internal "colony." In 1972 Robert Blauner, a native of Chicago and a sociologist who earned his PhD in 1962 from Berkeley, published *Racial Oppression in America*, which presents a theory of internal colonialism. This theory is a crystallization of the analysis of Black political dissidents and intellectuals such as the Black Panther's radicals, who had argued for years before this was published that Blacks (like Native Americans) had been "colonized." The Weather Underground identified the Black struggle as part of the "worldwide fight against US imperialism," and argued that the Black community's role in that struggle was of primary importance.

> If the Black community (or colony, as the Weatherman preferred to call it) was successful in its fight for liberation, the United States would not survive because of the essential role played by the citizens in the Black colony in the formation and perpetuation of the U.S. system. Slavery was fundamental to the development of capitalist society in the British colonies and in the first several decades of the United States: not only did the slave trade create profits which could be invested elsewhere, it also enabled slave owners to acquire wealth rapidly. When slavery was no longer essential to the continued accumulation of wealth, the ex-slaves and their descendants were relegated to a no less essential but often harsher economic slavery which existed to this day.
>
> (Jacobs 1997: 27)

Bernadine Dohrn, one of the co-founders of Weatherman and one of the drafters of the founding statement, represents White women who came to believe that armed struggle and insurrection against the United States was necessary to achieve their revolutionary goals. In a context of state violence, government repression against the student movement, the civil rights movement, the anti-war movement, and the Black Power movement, some feminists and non-feminist political activists saw violence as an appropriate response to state violence and used it in their struggle against the **Vietnam War**, U.S. imperialism, racism, and the forms of capitalism that kept some groups permanently impoverished and disempowered. A number of White women, including well-known revolutionaries such as Bernadine Dohrn, who self-identified as feminists and were members of the New Left, armed themselves and participated in violent armed struggles. Their motivations for arming themselves and using weapons were inspired by political ideologies regarding social justice, anti-imperialism, and anti-capitalism. They were engaged in what they considered to be emancipatory political action.

> New Leftists were not only implicitly united across national boundaries by their shared opposition to oppression, their commitment to democratic participation,

and their use of militant direct action as a means of protest, they were consciously internationalist. In what amounted to a global crusade, students and youth throughout the world protested the Vietnam War. They assimilated dimensions of Black Power and Third World revolutionary ideologies…. They created an international protest culture organized around master texts, chiefly those of Karl Marx, Mao Tse-tung, Herbert Marcuse, and "revolutionary" icons like Che Guevara and Ho Chi Minh.

(Varon 2004: 1)

Although the vast majority of political activists rejected violence as a political strategy, there were some groups who felt that violence was a legitimate and necessary political strategy in their struggle against what they perceived as an American empire exploiting the Third World and engaging in inhumane and morally unjust wars. The U.S. government was also using increasingly violent tactics against political dissidents, racial minorities, and others who were fighting for civil rights, racial justice, and participatory democracy.

Armed women held a prominent place in the … Weatherman, which had its genesis as an offshoot of the Students for a Democratic Society…. Spurred to acts of violence by their despair over the escalating conflict in Vietnam and as a means of helping oppressed people of color in the United States, Weatherman embraced theorist Regis Debray's theory of exemplary violence, … As former Weatherman leader Jeff Jones put it, he and his comrades learned from Debray that "a small group of very politically advanced, ideologically committed people can carry out revolutionary actions that will serve as an inspiration for other people." This strategy ran counter to more traditional forms of organizing.

(Browder 2006: 171)

White radical women on the left were often expected to prove that they were "tough". In the words of the Bread and Roses collective,

Women in the Weatherman are thus forced into a double bind. Not only are they told that their oppression, which they share with all other women, is less important or compelling than the oppression of blacks or Vietnamese, but their revolutionary commitment is measured by male chauvinist standards; they must struggle in terms defined by men. A woman becomes a heroine in Weather circles when she is a tougher, better fighter than the men, regardless of whether she's helping women's liberation.

(Browder 2006: 173)

The United States vs. Patricia Campbell Hearst

On February 4, 1974, **Patty Hearst**, the 19-year-old daughter of Randolph Hearst and an art major at the University of California, Berkeley (UC-Berkeley), was kidnapped at gunpoint by members of the *Symbionese Liberation Army* from her home in Berkeley, where she lived with her fiancé Steven Weed, a graduate student in philosophy. The daughter of the managing editor of the *San Francisco Examiner* and the granddaughter of William Randolph Hearst (the founder of the Hearst publishing empire), she belonged to one of the wealthiest and most powerful families in the United States.

Patricia Hearst had been targeted by members of the SLA and identified initially as a possible candidate for a "prisoner exchange" for Russ Little and Joseph Rimero who were incarcerated for the killing of Dr. Marcus Foster, the first Black school superintendent of the Oakland Public Schools. They were sent to San Quentin State Prison within 48 hours of the SLA propaganda being discovered in their safe house in Concord, California.

Ten weeks after her abduction, Patty Hearst had become a guerrilla fighter who self-identified as "Tania," a gun-toting "revolutionary feminist," and a member of the Symbionese Liberation Army. After participating in the robbery of a Hibernia branch bank in San Francisco, Hearst and her comrades fled with $10,960 in cash. Holding a semi-automatic carbine rifle, Patty Hearst was filmed by the automatic cameras in the bank. This image, which circulated in the national press and mesmerized the nation, transformed Hearst from a wealthy apolitical university student who had been kidnapped to an outlaw, a political dissident, and a member of a revolutionary political group. Her transformation generated anxieties about the central role that White upper-middle-class university students could play in the radical wings of the New Left organizations.

> On April 15, cameras inside the branch of Hibernia Bank at Noriega and Twenty-Second streets in San Francisco captured Patty Hearst with a shoulder-strapped carbine—perhaps loaded and ready to fire, perhaps not—pointed at bank employees. She was ringed by SLA comrades, whose guns, Patty's defense would argue, were trained on her. In the course of the robbery, Patty was to make a short speech, one that would convince the public that Patty Hearst was there, robbing a bank, and that she hadn't been brainwashed.
>
> (Graebner 2010: 24)

As an outlaw and media celebrity wanted by the FBI, Patty Hearst became a complicated symbol of an armed dissident and a White urban guerilla girl. An heiress to a publishing fortune who was raised on an estate by nannies and the granddaughter of one of the most powerful media tycoons in the United States, Patty Hearst was not the type of White girl destined to become a political radical, revolutionary feminist, fugitive, and bank robber. The U.S. media was not accustomed to seeing a privileged

White woman of her class background functioning as a talking head—a spokesperson for the Symbionese Liberation Army whose political projects included feeding the poor, prisoner rights, and tackling racism. As her distressed parents continued to define her as a kidnap victim who was under the influence of mind control, she participated in another bank robbery and lived underground with several other members of the Symbionese Liberation Army.

After 19 months of having robbed banks and living underground as a fugitive, Patty Hearst was arrested in San Francisco and taken into custody on September 18, 1975. She stood trial in January of 1976 for bank robbery and became an instant media celebrity. She was charged with 22 counts of federal and state violations including the Federal Firearms Act. Initially after her arrest, she referred to herself as an "urban guerrilla" and a "revolutionary feminist." When booked into the San Mateo County Jail, she listed "urban guerilla" as her occupation.

The trial of Patty Hearst was about more than her participation in a bank robbery. It was a proxy for a national debate that asked how affluent White girls became armed insurgents, anti-racist and anti-capitalist political dissidents. How did it happen? Four psychiatrists, one each from Stanford, UC-Berkeley, UCLA, and the University of Southern California, were asked to evaluate Patty Hearst and were given tapes of private conversations that she had with friends who visited her and her affadavit taken several days after she was arrested.

The question that mesmerized the nation, the media, and the jury was "Who was the 'real' Patty Hearst?" Was she an heiress who had been brainwashed and lost her ability to think rationally? Or had she really become someone else? Had she become a political radical, a White anti-racist who was concerned about poverty and prison conditions? Was she responsible for what she did or was she in an altered state? Were there two Patty Hearsts? Which one was responsible (in charge of her consciousness) when she participated in the bank robbery? The brainwashed kidnap victim or the revolutionary feminist? Which Patty was on trial? The engaged college student who was apolitical or the post-kidnapped Patty who had become sympathetic to the causes of the poor, Blacks, Vietnamese, and political radicals? How did the change occur? Was it voluntary? Had she been tortured or brainwashed?

On March 20, 1976, Patty Hearst was convicted of bank robbery and sentenced to 35 years in prison. After having served 22 months, President Jimmy Carter commuted her sentence and she was released on February 19, 1979.

DISCUSSION QUESTIONS

1. The modern-day guns rights movement owes a debt to the Black Panther Party. Explain how the activities of the Black Panther Party redefined the symbolic and political meaning and use of guns by Black wo/men? What impact did this have on gun legislation?

2. Explain how the Black Panther's conceptualization of the relationship between gun ownership and citizenship compares with the position of the National Rifle Association?

3. Select a memoir or a section of a memoir written by a White female member of the Weather Underground and one by a female member of the Black Panther Party (e.g. Bernadine Dohrn and Elaine Brown). Compare and contrast their analysis of weapons. How do they describe their political philosophy regarding their use of guns *as women* and as *revolutionaries* who participated in what they defined as anti-imperial, social justice, and/or racial justice political projects?

III: The Mommy Wars

The National Debate on Gun Regulation

O n August 10, 1999, an armed gunman entered the North Valley Jewish Community Center during a summer day-camp program and opened fire in Granada Hills, California. One month earlier a White supremacist murdered Ricky Byrdsong, a Black basketball coach at Northwestern University, and then began shooting people who were leaving a synagogue in the Chicago suburbs. Thirteen children were killed on April 18, 2000 by two White teenage gunmen in Littleton, Colorado. After a series of shootings revealed and demonstrated the ease with which people (particularly White male teenagers) could purchase and secure deadly weapons without a license, background check, or restrictions on quantity of guns, a movement for increased regulation of guns took off led by a White mother.

In the aftermath of a wave of school shootings in the United States perpetrated by White adolescent males and/or White male militiamen, a polarizing debate about firearms restrictions was renewed and circulated in the national press. The "social life" of the gun became a central part of the gun debates. Was the gun "nice" and polite and harmless or was it "aggressive" and dangerous? In other words, different types of gun were described as having social characteristics, personalities, and were classified as "good" or "bad"—qualities that we often associated with living beings. In the words of Deborah Homsher:

> Partisan political groups in the United States have identified two essential, but contradictory, aspects of a gun: pro-gunners insist that guns are inert tools … while anti-gunners maintain that they are active, alluring agents. This disagreement raises questions not only about the *real* identity of a gun, but about the composition of the American people…. In the late 1990s, this political definition of a gun's—particularly a handgun's—"identity" as a public health hazard sparked a new anti-gun initiative as cities throughout the United States began to file suits against gun dealers and manufacturers for the damage sustained as a result of these "unsafe" products and the gun industry's allegedly irresponsible sale and distribution policies.
>
> (2001: 10–11)

The issue of arming women generated debates that divided feminists and non-feminists alike. Feminist opponents of arming women drew on arguments that were demeaning and compared women to children. In *Gun Women: Firearms and Feminism in Contemporary America*, Mary Zeiss Stange and Carol K. Oyster argue that some feminist opponents have recycled stereotypes about women in their arguments:

> As gullible as children, women are unable to resist the lure of advertisements that offer the "false sense of security" of gun ownership. Even granting that women are appropriately afraid, they are deluded into trying to defend themselves when they should depend upon others to protect them.... On this issue most feminists have perpetuated the same age-old gender stereotypes of female weakness and vulnerabilities that they quite rightly reject in other political and social contexts. The result is an odd set of cognitive dissonance. Women who know perfectly well otherwise are willing to take as established fact that gun-armed women are naïve, childlike, and/or competent. It doesn't add up.
>
> (2000: 62–63)

Mothers concerned about the safety of their children versus mothers who believe that they had the "right" to arm themselves assumed positions as spokespersons and marshaled evidence to support their positions on opposing sides of the debate about the need for increased regulations and restrictions of handguns. However, the increased number of women being trained by the U.S. Armed Forces in the use of lethal weapons and the everyday violence that poor children, particularly Black and Brown Latinos in urban areas, encountered was not part of the debate. The debates centered on two questions: First, who is responsible for the safety and protection of women and children—the individual or the federal government? The second question was "Should the government intervene and make it more difficult to obtain fire arms or is there already sufficient legislation at the local and state level regulating gun sales?"

The Million Mom March

In *Looking For a Few Good Moms*, Donna Dees-Thomases, a 42-year-old White mother of two and a public relations consultant, describes what motivated her to found and organize the **Million Mom March**, which was held in 2000. The Million Mom March has been described as the largest mass demonstration in support of gun control in U.S. history. Ms. Dees-Thomases directly challenged the gun industry and powerful

National Rifle Association lobby, which has successfully lobbied against increased federal regulation of gun sales or restrictions on sales, including "commonsense" gun regulations such as requiring all guns to be registered, all gun owners to be licensed, and background checks to be carried out prior to the sale of any firearms.

While vacationing with her family on Fire Island, Ms. Dees-Thomases learned of the Granada Hills shooting, one of several shootings that summer, while watching the national news.

> I was immobilized with shock. I stayed with the program and watched in horror as the television camera zoomed out to show the powerful images of SWAT teams leading these preschoolers off to safety. The program then cut to two law-enforcement officials, one from Vancouver, the other from Seattle, who tried to apply reason to this insanity. Handguns and assault weapons, they both said, were much too easy to get in this country, especially compared with Canada where the laws were much stricter.
>
> (Dees-Thomases and Hendrie 2004: 3)

In *The Times*, the U.S. gun debates and the planned Million Mom March was characterized by Ben McIntyre in these words:

> Mothers are the most revered demographic in American life, and the "soccer moms", once considered the key to election success, have been elbowed aside this year by gun-concerned Moms. Some 72 percent of American women favor greater regulation of guns compared to just 22 percent of men—that is a statistic politicians anxious to get elected in 2000 will ignore at their peril.
>
> (2000)

On May 14, 2000, Mother's Day, the largest mass demonstration in the United States since the Vietnam War, occurred in the nation's capital. It brought together more than 500,000 mothers, fathers, grandparents, and children in the Washington Mall. The goal of this demonstration was to send a clear signal to Congress during an election year in which several mass shootings had occurred including the Columbine shooting by two White teenage boys armed with semi automatic weapons. The demonstrators wanted Congress to pass "common sense gun regulation."

The Million Mom March was a display of collective action by mothers which used the logics and language of "**maternalism**" that had been used 80 years earlier by suffragists arguing for women's right to vote. Mothers proved to be a formidable grass-roots political constituency advocating for increased regulation of the firearms industry. Critics have argued that they employed rhetoric and logics that were not unlike those of the "gunners," or pro-gun women's groups.

In *Women & Guns: Politics and the Culture of Firearms in America*, Deborah Homsher presents the voices of women who are pro- and anti-gun advocates. Homsher interviewed women in the 1990s who held divergent attitudes and opposing political positions on gun regulation and ownership in the United States. Summarizing the U.S. national debates about gun ownership and the way the women were deployed as political symbols in the mainstream media, Homsher notes that:

> Often these debates featured women as *women*, for instance, as bereaved mothers or wives, who could advocate effectively for stricter gun-control laws, or as potential victims who could advocate effectively for the "right to carry" legislation that would allow them to carry concealed handguns in public for personal self-defense.
>
> (2001: 4)

Safely in Mother's Arms: A Women's Pro-Gun Organization

> You think as a mother, you want to protect your children and I think children should feel safe in their mother's arms.... And the arms being a double entendre because you have a call to arms, being prepared and those sorts of things.
>
> (Alicia Waldas)

You are at a party. One of the other guests presents you with a loaded firearm. Do you know what to do? Have you been taught how to safely and quickly disarm a handgun, a revolver, a rifle? Alicia Waldas believes that women and children should be taught how to safely disarm firearms and offers a curriculum that would prepare you for this situation.

> So my stance is that if you decide, as a woman, that part of your protection is to use a firearm, then I'm going to make sure that you go and get properly educated and train regularly with it and that you teach your children firearm safety.... We are not making a judgement that you should or shouldn't use it—that it's good or it's bad.
>
> (Alicia Waldas, interview transcript)

The Founder and President of **Safely in Mother's Arms**, Alicia Waldas is the mother of three children, who describes herself as "a working mother and, at the time, single mother." Born in 1956 in Minnesota, Waldas, who is 55 years old, lives with her family in Phoenix, Arizona and has been a gun owner for 16 years (since 1995). She founded Safely in Mother's Arms in 2000 and remains the President of this organization which has members in 36 states. In an interview conducted on July 13, 2011, when asked what motivated her to found the organization Ms. Waldas replied:

There were so many things going on in the world that I had not prepared my children to defend themselves against. If you recall, the whole Columbine School thing happened … I had to think about what would I advise my children to do had they been in that situation. And that began my personal search for how would I teach my children to protect themselves in a real situation…. You know the police are not our personal body guards and they couldn't respond to something that was already happening anyway…. And what I found was a dearth of information. It was … heavy, heavy law enforcement kind of thing. There was nothing practical or in the middle. I needed to do something.

Safely in Mother's Arms is an all-volunteer organization and has no paid employees. And Waldas is careful to characterize her organization as not promoting gun consumption, rather in her words:

Mother's Arms doesn't officially have a stand on advocating gun ownership because we don't. What we do advocate is gun safety and teaching our children about firearms and how to be safe around them. That was part of why I founded the organization. I, frankly, was petrified of firearms … I live in Arizona. I have three children and when they were all babies I taught them how to swim because there were so many drowning here in Arizona. I began to realize gun safety was just one more thing that I needed to do on my check-off list.

Safely in Mother's Arms offers classes and workshops. Waldas now operates primarily through organizations such as churches, schools, corporations, and community organizations. Below she describes a curriculum that she developed called "First Defense":

It's basically what to do until the first responders arrive. And it covers a wide variety of topics for everyday life: traveling to and from in your car, if you use public transportation, if you work in a high rise building, if you're on vacation, if you travel for business … what to do if you're in your home and you have a home invasion, and so forth…. I customized my First Defense program to what a social worker and a case worker would need to know.

Although Ms. Waldas doesn't explicitly mention race, her analysis of the historical origins of women with arms calls upon the image of "pioneer" women who were typically represented as Europeans or European Americans, excluding Native American, Black, Chinese, or Japanese women on the frontier.

Waldas has been conducting classes primarily for corporations, church organizations, rotary clubs, and mothers' clubs. In her words, "What I'm finding most recently to be most successful is that I teach it to corporations that do education for their employees. I've done it at Ford Motor Company … I taught the Navajo, American Indian social workers/case worker."

In the absence of systematic research on women who participate in gun-training classes it is not possible to determine the degree to which Safely in Mother's Arms is representative of other gun-training organizations in the United States. However, the discourse that circulates about the services being provided to women that is published by gun advocacy groups reveals a number of problems that divert attention away from racial and class inequalities between women and the way that power inequalities structure women's relationship to guns. In Waldas's analysis, she notes that:

> What is interesting to me is that when I look at it from a historical perspective, … in the prairie days women were so self-sufficient and self-reliant. It was just as comfortable for them to have a shot gun sitting next to the cabin door as it was to have a skillet on the stove … Why did, in the interest of becoming "civilized," did we, as women, lose some of our self-reliance?

Who has privileged access to guns and weapons training? For civilian women this depends in part on where one resides, one's economic resources (to pay for classes and weapons), and the political and social organizations in the community. Waldas reports that only about 1 percent of the women served are Black, yet Blacks make up roughly 12 percent of the U.S. population and Black women form roughly half of all enlisted women in the U.S. Army. However, they are also concentrated among the poor and working poor. Women from middle- and upper-middle-class backgrounds, women who have the financial resources, can purchase handguns that range in price from $500.

The Smith & Wesson catalog advertises a revolver named the Home Defense Kit, a low-capacity pistol that has 10+1 rounds for $499 excluding tax. For poor women or stay-at-home mothers, who do not have their own income and may not have husbands who support their owning a gun, this sum would be prohibitive. The issue of who has the resources (financial) and the ability to purchase guns and the time to go to a shooting range and take classes is not addressed by these organizations. There is also an assumption that all women are equally at risk. But women who are employed and are able to leave their homes and have networks of support outside of their immediate family may have access to sources of power that other women lack.

Black women have lower rates of gun ownership when compared with White women. Despite the significance of race, gender, and poverty in shaping one's emotional, historical, and social relationship (and economic access) to the firearms industry and the small arms (handgun) market, as evident by the fact that White men continue to be the core market, the gun advocacy propaganda literature tends to universalize the experiences of women and men, collapsing differences in income (class inequality), race/ethnicity, age, and region. Violence against women is discussed without regard to the systematic violence that Black women, American Indian women, and poor women have faced, which included state-sanctioned violence that did not only involve intimate partners. The racial and class hierarchies that exist among women are not acknowledged or mentioned in the debates on gun regulations.

In a study of the "lifetime risk" of being a victim of homicide, race is a significant factor with Blacks being exposed to higher rates of gun violence. Deborah Prothrow-Stith, a physician and an assistant dean of the Harvard School of Public Health, compared the White and Black, male and female "lifetime risk" for homicide in the United States and concluded that "if the risk a white female incurs is set at 1, then the risk for white males would measure 2.4 (more than twice as likely to be murdered), black females 4.2 and black males are 18.4 times more likely to be victims of homicide" (as quoted in Homsher 2001: 162). Yet pro-gun groups do not appear to be aggressively courting Black women and men as potential consumers who might need guns to protect themselves. Deborah Homsher interviewed Black women in poor communities such as Camden, New Jersey, an area with a high crime rate. Homsher compares these women to the White "frontier women" in the past. She writes:

> [T]he African American women I met who worked and lived in public housing in Camden seemed to understand very well the reality of living on the edge of a *frontier*.... Their fatalism was intermixed with an abiding sense of attachment, not only to their children, but also to their neighborhoods, where they had lived for many years, refusing to flee despite an accumulation of terrible events, including the maiming, by gunfire, of their sons' arms, legs, and chests. To my mind, this mix of fatalism and attachment characterizes a prototypical frontier voice.
>
> (2001: 163)

We learn from Homsher's research that Black women whose children had been victims of violent gun-related crime differed from White women in their politics as "conservative" in their views about gun regulation.

> None of them expressed interest in legislation that would make it easier for citizens to acquire concealed-carry permits. None of them, in short, showed faith in the proposition that putting guns in the hands of law-abiding neighborhood residents would intimidate criminals and ultimately reduce neighborhood violence.
>
> (2001: 163)

The African American women with whom I spoke ... lacked, however, certain kinds of economic and civil power that many Americans inherit without much effort.... Camden's women lived in a city so empty of job opportunities that the landscape had become surreal. And they lived divided from the men one would expect to husband and help them over time.... In a way, this meant that they lived inside an exaggerated version of an old American dream that directs men out into the wilderness with their guns and instructs the women to stay home with the children.

(2001: 183)

Shannon Frattaroli, a researcher at the Johns Hopkins Center for Gun Policy Research, located in East Baltimore, identifies what she sees as a paradox in the way that race, poverty, and residence affect which women decide to arm themselves. In an interview with Caitlin Kelly, Frattaroli identifies a racial pattern in gun ownership that is consistent with the Gallup polls.

Frattaroli, who is white, says the black women she knows facing gun violence are not rushing to arm themselves. "They're *not* afraid. They see the downsides of a culture saturated with guns, and they're suffering terribly for it." Frattaroli points out that women who have the least to fear—suburban whites in safe neighborhoods—often choose to arm themselves, while we're immersed in this culture of fear, the women we'd suspect who would feel the most vulnerable are the toughest and the least fearful.

(Kelly 2004: 111)

Black people are disproportionately poor when compared to Whites, Asians, and White Latinos. They are residentially concentrated in hyper-segregated communities where violence is more prevalent—both from the police and from other residents. The paradox is that Blacks are more likely than their White peers to support gun regulation and to be opposed to relaxing gun laws because they tend to live in urban communities where gun violence and crime are serious problems, like the District of Columbia.

In addition to racial disparities that Frattoli found in gun ownership among women, researchers have found a number of regional disparities in terms of gun ownership and gun violence among women. For example, Caitlin Kelly found that:

[A] 1996 study compared murders in three Southern cities—Atlanta, Baltimore and Houston with New York, Chicago, and Los Angeles.... A major regional disparity also became clear: Southern women were far more likely to shoot to kill—60.1 percent versus 39.9 percent of Northern women (perhaps because guns are more easy to obtain in the three Southern States studied....)

(2004: 133)

The Second Amendment

The landmark case *District of Columbia v. Heller* challenged the city's 32-year-old ban on all functional firearms in the home. Handguns could not be licensed or registered in D.C. This ban on guns was overturned by the U.S. Supreme Court and was seen as "reviving the Second Amendment." In June 2008 the Supreme Court ruled in a 5–4 decision that D.C.'s gun ban was unconstitutional and violated the Second Amendment Since the ratification of the Second Amendment in 1791, the Court had not conclusively interpreted the gun rights issue. This court decision also struck down Washington, D.C.'s requirement that firearms be equipped with trigger locks or kept disassembled.

In the aftermath of this decision, residents living in the safest and wealthiest suburban neighborhoods outside of D.C. began registering guns that they had purchased. In an editorial published in the *Washington Post* in August 2008, we learn that "[r]esidents in Washington's safest, most well-to-do neighborhoods have armed themselves far more than 'people in poorer' crime plagued areas" (*Washington Post* 2008: A16). This is one of the contradictions and ironies. Why would wealthy White people living in safe neighborhoods arm themselves while poor Blacks are less likely to do so? Could it be that having first-hand experience with violence generates a distrust of anyone armed and there is a lack of faith that well-meaning people who arm themselves will not harm you?

Intimate Partner Violence

One of the arguments consistently made by the pro-gun lobby and women who oppose stricter regulation of firearms sales is that guns enable women to empower themselves—to defend themselves against a potential rapist or home intruder. Perhaps this has some merit for women living in communities where there are high incidences of home burglaries and break-ins—but the research has shown that women are more

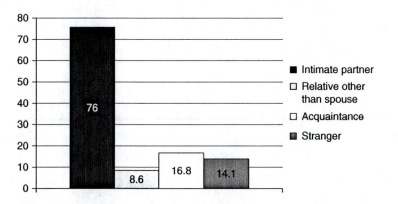

Figure 3.1 Percentage of adult rape victims by victim–perpetrator relationship.
Source: U.S. Department of Justice, November 1998. Prepared by Melissa MacDonald.

at risk from intimate partners living in their homes. While there are clearly situations in which a gun could be effectively used by a woman to defend herself, it is also the case that in both the civilian and the military populations, women are typically assaulted by people whom they know or with whom they work. In the case of female soldiers, their memoirs, testimonies, and **Department of Defense** reports reveal that serving in the Armed Forces and knowing how to effectively use weapons did not protect female soldiers from **sexual assault** in their platoons.

Who one imagines to be the threat is an issue that divides women who are proponents of stricter gun regulation from those who oppose increased firearms regulation. If your husband, female partner, family member, or close friend is the person you should fear, will having a gun protect you? Women who are motivated by fear of crime to purchase and learn to effectively use guns are typically imagining a stranger, a home intruder, but what if the person who subjects you to violence is your spouse, domestic partner, boyfriend, girlfriend, or family member? How do you defend yourself against an **intimate partner**, that is, a person with whom you live, cohabit, or who has access to your home?

In a study conducted by the U.S. Justice Department in 2000, one of the major findings is the degree to which women are victimized by people they know rather than strangers. **Intimate partner violence** is a bigger threat to most U.S. women than stranger violence, which means that arming oneself may not protect one against your spouse, domestic partner, boyfriend, father, brother, or relative. In fact, intimate partners pose a greater threat to women than previously thought. According to this report, "[t]he data show that violence is more widespread and injurious to women's and men's health than previously thought—an important finding for legislators, policymakers, intervention planners and researchers" (2000: iii).

Women who live in the most dangerous neighborhoods often do not have the resources to buy a $500 Home Protection Kit and pay for a license, gun classes, and other accessories. In other words the women who may be the most in need of protection from home intruders are the least likely to purchase guns, or to have the resources to purchase a handgun. They may also live in those cities, regions, and communities with the most restrictive gun legislation so it may be more difficult for them to purchase a handgun when compared with their suburban or rural White peers.

DISCUSSION QUESTIONS

1. If Black women typically live in poorer neighborhoods and are at greater risk of homicide, why are they less likely to own guns and be pro-gun than their White female suburban peers? Explain how poverty, race, and residential segregation play a role in attitudes towards gun violence.
2. You have been hired to recruit teenage girls into a new gun-training program by a local gun sales distributor. However, you do not want to alienate the parents

(particularly the mothers) at the school who are in favor of increased gun regulation so you need to advocate for free gun-training classes without encouraging gun purchasing. How would you approach this task? Present two arguments in support of the need for weapons training for teenage girls and two arguments in support of increased gun regulations and restrictions on gun purchases for teenagers.

IV: Firearms Feminism and Militarized Femininity

In the popular imagination, these firearms have always been, and belonged, in male hands....

(Stange and Oyster 2000: 22)

What happens when women enter the masculinist spaces of the military and war zones? Are the women masculinized, are the spaces feminized, or does something else occur?

(Feitz and Nagel 2008: 201)

The **United States Military Academy**, known as West Point, was established by Congress in 1802 to train the officers and military leaders of the U.S. Armed Forces. West Point excluded women until 1976, thus denying them an opportunity to receive the weapons training that they would need to become military leaders. For more than 150 years the state-sanctioned exclusion of women from military academies remained unchallenged. This masculine-only military institution reinforced masculine privilege and occupational sex segregation by defining "heroic" occupations such as military leadership as exclusively masculine and as central to citizenship.

[T]he service academies admitted only men, in obeisance to a pervasive assumption that men alone could lead and fight in combat. By the 1970s, however, almost all assumptions about women were under intense pressure on a national scale, and the rapid pace of cultural change led Congress to use the military, and ultimately the academies, to offer greater opportunities to American women. When legislators opened these institutions to women in 1976, they did so to advance the cause of equality ... this revolutionary event *was* a critical step towards placing women in direct combat positions.

(Janda 2000: 305)

Joan Acker, a feminist sociologist, has described the military as a **gendered institution**. In defining a gendered institution, Acker notes that:

gender is present in the processes, practices, images and ideologies and distributions of power in the various sectors of social life. Taken as more or less functioning wholes, the institutional structures of the US and other societies are organized along lines of gender.... These institutions have been defined by the absence of women.

(1992: 567)

Gender in this case refers to gendered inequalities that result in differences in rank, power, and authority.

Until the end of the 20th century, the military academies resembled the Catholic priesthood and prisons. The Armed Forces were institutional spaces where men spent most of their time with other men in all-male domains. The military workforce was a male domain where women only entered as "temporary" laborers, auxiliary support staff, or providers of pleasure. They were not viewed (or treated) as equal members or potential leaders and were not trained to be competent in weapons use until the 1970s.

Military service has historically been tied to masculinity and full citizenship in the United States, a nation where women did not have the right to vote until 1920. The military was an arena where men, particularly combat veterans, could prove their loyalty to the nation and be rewarded with the highest honors. It is also an institution where **gender ideologies** about female fragility and consequently gender equality were reproduced. By defining women as a class of citizens that must be "protected" from military service and armed combat (except during a labor shortage) while requiring men to enlist, one of the occupations perceived as the most dangerous and thus "heroic" was reserved for men.

During the revolutionary period when the United States was still a British colony, women were not actively recruited to fight in wars. However, some women concealed their sex and employed **gender camouflage** to enlist and thus serve in all-male army units. Disguised as a man, Deborah Samson was the first female soldier in the U.S. Army. Born in 1760 she fought alongside men in the Continental Army without being discovered or revealing her sex.

At the age of twenty-two, Samson, a schoolteacher, disguised herself in men's clothing and hiked to Boston, where she enlisted in the Continental Army under the name Robert Shurtleff. She served for over a year in the Fourth Massachusetts Regiment and was commended as an outstanding officer.... [S]he received an honorable discharge—given the money to travel home by General George Washington himself—and settled in Sharon, Massachusetts, where she married a farmer, Benjamin Gannet, and had three children.... Dressed in her old army uniform, she would give a short lecture about her military adventures, then dazzle the audience with a precision rifle drill. Finally in 1792, at the urging of her friend and neighbor Paul Revere, she applied for and received veteran's benefits.

(Kelly 2004: 56)

After World War II, members of the Senate including Dennis Chavez, a Democrat representing New Mexico, initiated discussions about establishing a military academy specifically for women. Feminists challenged the practice of **occupational segregation** by gender and advocated that women should be allowed to enter all-male universities and military academies. Denied training at the military academies, until recently female soldiers were not able to qualify for leadership positions or to serve in the highest ranks of the military.

From Typewriter Soldiers to Armed Soldiers

On June 12, 1948 President Harry Truman signed the legislation that established a permanent place for women in the Army, Navy, Air Force, and Marines. Prior to this, women were perceived primarily as "temporary" and auxiliary labor to be used in administrative, clerical, or medical capacities as secretaries, nurses, laundresses, or cooks. The Women's Armed Services Act, which was passed by Congress in a vote of 206 to 133, was interpreted in multiple ways. For female veterans it was a recognition and validation of the service that they had given to their country while for feminists it was viewed as a step towards gender equality in the military even though it provided limited opportunities for women to serve in peace-time service.

President John F. Kennedy established the **Commission on the Status of Women** and appointed Eleanor Roosevelt (former first lady and the widow of Franklin Delano Roosevelt) to chair it, in December 1961. During his announcement of this new committee which led to the 1963 Equal Pay Act, Kennedy stated "Women should not be considered a marginal group to be employed periodically only to be denied the opportunity to satisfy their needs and aspirations when unemployment rises or a war ends." Although this presidential rhetoric did not lead to immediate changes in the status of women in the U.S. Armed Forces, it did reflect vigorous debates that were occurring about how and under what conditions to include women as "permanent" members of the Armed Forces.

In a 1966 *Washington Post* article, women Marines were referred to as "typewriter soldiers" and characterized as being more concerned with "the arts of makeup than the arts of war" (Jack Anderson, quoted in Holm 1982: 190). Femininity and physical appearance were central in the training of new recruits in the U.S. Air Force and the Army in the early 1960s. Jeannie Holm, a retired major-general in the U.S. Air Force, spent 33 years serving in the Armed Forces during a period of policy changes as women slowly became more integrated into non-combat positions. She describes how gender ideologies structured the type of basic training that new female recruits received:

> The obsession with appearance carried over to all aspects of the women's programs. For example, except for the uniforms and the marching, the indoctrination programs more closely resembled ladies' finishing schools than military programs. Military aspects of training considered too masculine were played down or eliminated, and subjects designed to enhance femininity and women's proper role in the military were emphasized.... Nor were they allowed any longer to take weapons familiarization courses or to fire small arms, even voluntarily, because these were considered a waste of training time and would detract from the image the Army wanted to project.
>
> (Holm 1982: 176–77)

On November 8, 1967 President Lyndon B. Johnson signed into law Public Law 90–130, which removed restrictions on the careers of female officers serving in the Army, Navy, Air Force, and Marine Corps. It was the first major policy change affecting women in the Armed Forces since 1947. Describing the motivations and events that led to these legislative changes despite the resistance to the full integration of women, Jeannie Holm writes:

> At the April **DACOWITS** (Defense Advisory Committee on Women In The Services) meeting, the DOD [Department of Defense] had briefed the committee on the growing demands for manpower to support the escalating war in Vietnam and the other troop deployments ... thousands of qualified women volunteers were being turned away and ... many recruits ... were being delayed for months in reporting for duty because of artificial ceilings on recruits.
>
> (1982: 190; bold added; see glossary)

This change in government policy removed a form of legalized or state-sanctioned discrimination that had barred women from occupations that had been previously defined as "male" unless there was a temporary labor shortage. Describing the elimination of this form of gender discrimination by the U.S. government, Summerfield identifies a paradox:

> Unlike so many other advances for women, this push to demolish the exclusive male hold on American service academies was not driven by mainstream feminist groups. They saw gender discrimination in the military as far less important than issues like equal pay and sexual harassment in the civilian workplace, which affected the majority of women. They were also divided as to whether military women were liberal-minded reformers attacking patriarchy or sell-outs to

a male-dominated institution that practiced violence and too often exploited women.

(2000: 315)

Female soldiers employed by the U.S. Armed Services become militarized. They are used and deployed as weapons of war. By enlisting in the Armed Services they have accepted what Max Weber calls the "legitimated" authority of the state and have agreed to carry out authorized acts of violence on behalf of the government. As state actors and employees of the U.S. Armed Services, their primary role is to support state-sanctioned violence as a way to resolve international conflicts.

The All-Volunteer Army: The Armed Forces Rediscover Women

In 1973 the U.S. government ended the **draft**, also known as conscription or compulsory military service, for men and shifted to an All-Volunteer Army. The Armed Forces became the nation's single largest employer of youth. Gender integration, that is the integration of women into all branches of the Armed Services (in non-combat units) began that same year. Describing the motivations for gender integration in the 1970s, Cynthia Enloe writes that "Fearing that an all-volunteer force would become disproportionately reliant on African-American men, "manpower" planners inside the Defense Department and in the powerful congressional armed services committees apparently looked to other sources for military recruits. They rediscovered women" (2000: 85). Lorry Fenner writes:

Only after military planners decided they could not recruit enough middle-class white men and the Civil Rights and Women's Movements changed the public's

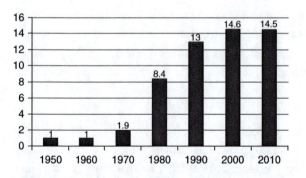

Figure 4.1 Percentage of women in the U.S. Military.
Source: Population Reference Bureau, December 2004, Statistics on Women in the Military, Women in Military Service for America Memorial Foundation, Inc., 2011.

conception of fairness in employment and opportunity did the Services turn to women. Because more women were needed, military leaders sought nontraditional areas in which they could contribute—the most nontraditional being combat positions. As we know, many nontraditional occupations have been opened to women over the past 20 years. The law only barred women from combat vessels and aircraft in the Navy and Air Force; the Army excluded women from combat positions by policy.

(Fenner and de Young 2001: 61)

Two years after the United States shifted to an All-Volunteer Army (and seven years after the Black Panthers were training women in firearms), women began receiving required weapons training for the first time. In the words of Jeannie Holm:

Beginning in 1975, the Army required all women to participate in individual weapons training. Enlisted women took to the firing range to learn basic rifle marksmanship and, during advanced individual training, learned to handle whatever weapon was required to meet the prerequisites of their specialities. Those assigned to combat support units learned to use the light antitank weapons, M-16 rifles, grenade launchers, claymore mines, and M-60 machine guns.

(1982: 273)

The historian Cynthia Enloe provides a trenchant analysis of one of the political paradoxes for military recruiters who need more women to enlist to fill the labor gap but are invested in the masculine culture of the military and resist any changes.

The recruitment of women is one of several strategies used by nations to fill the ranks of the military as described by Enloe. These include: 1) the draft, the conscription of men as a citizenship requirement; 2) volunteer soldiering; 3) contracting out military service to civilian and private agencies (outsourcing); 4) hiring foreign mercenaries; 5) kidnapping male children and forcing them to serve; 6) enlisting women. The enlistment of women poses specific challenges to the hypermasculine culture of the military. Enloe describes the struggle to maintain the masculine organizational culture of the military:

When those officials still committed to a masculinized military decide to travel down a sixth recruitment path—deliberately enlisting women into the ranks—they proceed as if they were performing a political high wire act. . . . they believe that they need to recruit and deploy women in only those ways that will not subvert the fundamentally masculinized culture of the military. To surrender its masculinized culture might result in few young men joining the ranks at all. Somehow, that is, the military that enlists women must remain, it is thought, a military that is appealing to men.... Moreover not too many women should achieve high rank.

And women recruits should not deprive men of the chance to serve in those posts held most precious to masculinity-seeking men.

(2000: 237–38)

Cultural Myths about Female Soldiers

One of the biggest cultural myths that civilians are exposed to in national debates about female soldiers serving in the U.S. Armed Services is that because women are technically banned from combat positions and do not engage in direct combat, they are exposed to less violence than their male colleagues. The evidence from the Department of Defense as well as memoirs by female soldiers contradict this belief. There is a tension between our belief in women's gendered vulnerability and the realities of modern war.

The idea that women do not commit violence and are primarily nurturers and therefore should not be allowed in combat positions is a cultural myth that Americans remain invested in and defend. This myth relies on gender ideologies that reinforce a gendered segregation, and **gendered division of labor** in the military (and male supremacy) by excluding women from positions in combat infantry, special operations, armor, artillery, and other positions that could lead to combat medals, promotions, and be converted into capital in the civilian world.

Gendered barriers are career obstacles that are implemented through policies that define some occupations and roles as "masculine." Combat has been defined as "masculine" and restricted to men. The official exclusion of women from combat positions reinforces the idea (gender ideology) that combat is an exclusively masculine activity and that heroism is reserved for men. This is an example of gender segregation within the military and it preserves male access to jobs that are higher status (as evidenced by war medals). Medals for heroism are typically given only to men who have served and/or been wounded in combat positions.

Scholars analyzing the experiences of women in war as well as memoirs by female soldiers demonstrate that the line between combatant and non-combatant is blurred in actual practice. In the words of Penny Summerfield:

In practice the distinction between combatant and non-combatant roles was hard to maintain because air attack, bombing and the threat of invasion dispersed the front line and brought it home. But the heroic status of the military civilian in wartime political rhetoric and popular culture polarized the two identities and increased the insecurity of the civilian.

(2000: 119)

Describing the controversy over arming women to fight as soldiers alongside men, Laura Browder reminds us that "Given the strong historical linkage between

Table 4.1 U.S. Army salary by rank: basic pay for active duty soldiers and officers, 2011 U.S. Army pay tables.

Rank	< 2 Years' Experience	4 Years' Experience	6 Years' Experience
Private (E1)	$17,611	–	–
Private (E2)	$19,739	$19,739	$19,739
Private First Class (E3)	$20,758	$23,400	$23,400
Specialist or Corporal (E4)	$22,993	$26,770	$27,911
Sergeant (E5)	$25,081	$29,380	$31,442
Staff Sergeant	$27,374	$32,742	$34,088
Second Lieutenant (O1)	$33,408	$42,030	$42,030
First Lieutenant (O2)	$38,488	$52,189	$53,262
Captain (O3)	$44,543	$59,422	$62,266

Source: U.S. Army website www.goarmy.com/benefits/money/basic-pay-active-duty-soldiers.html.

citizenship and the right and obligation to fight in wars, the female soldier has been a particularly contested figure in United States history" (2006: 15).

In *Creating G.I. Jane*, a historical analysis of the Women's Army Corps during World War II, Lisa Meyer offers a thoughtful analysis of the campaign waged to get the public to accept women as "auxiliaries" in the Armed Forces. The concern over women's hetero(sexuality) and the efforts to control and regulate their behavior is a focus of this book. We also learn from Meyer that women were trained in weapons' use and that their experiences were complex. In her words:

> I do not contest that the military is among the most powerful masculine institutions, or that women's entrance into and interaction with it present dangers and sometimes insurmountable difficulties. Yet, military women, during World War II, did not and do not perceive themselves as exclusively victims. Women's reasons for entering the military were and remain complex, and their struggles to obtain legitimacy in bastions of male power. The increasing number of young women, especially African American women, who are entering the military for jobs, education, or as a career, underlies the need to historicize both American women's role in the US military and the process by which G.I. Jane or the female soldier was created and continues to be constructed.
>
> (1998: 5)

There are multiple pathways to service in the military. For the White daughters and granddaughters of career officers, their service is a continuation of a formerly male lineage of distinguished and honorable citizenship while for first-generation or "new" Americans, it may be a distinguished and respectable path to citizenship; for poor tenth-generation U.S.-born Blacks it may be one of the few routes out of poverty and to a respectable job and education.

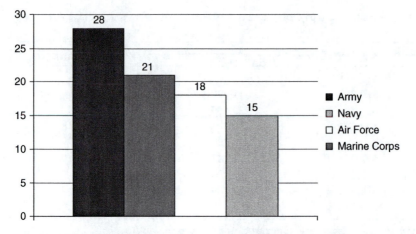

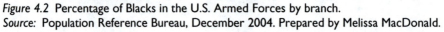

Figure 4.2 Percentage of Blacks in the U.S. Armed Forces by branch.
Source: Population Reference Bureau, December 2004. Prepared by Melissa MacDonald.

How have female soldiers been represented in popular culture? And why does this matter? The growing numbers of actual female soldiers and their increased visibility has been accompanied by a parallel increase in media representations in Hollywood films, television shows, as well as advertisements. According to Lisa Meyer:

> In fact, the most resilient and entrenched historical images of female soldiers are those of the camp follower and cross-dresser.... The historic image of female soldiers as cross-dressers was also articulated during World War II in public allegations that the WAC both attracted and produced "mannish" women. The mannish woman was a cultural symbol of lesbians prior to the war.... Both female and male military leaders, as well as civilian proponents of the women's corps, agreed that "female soldiers" must not seem to threaten either male power in the military nor the notion that masculinity was integrally tied to the definition of "soldier."

(1998: 7)

The U.S. Armed Services and Hollywood films have been a theater for the performance of masculinity and femininity. During the last decades of the 20th century and the first decade of the 21st century, media representations of femininity have been expanded to accommodate the increase in armed women, particularly women employed by local, state, or federal governments to serve as police detectives, soldiers, and officers.

In the media depictions of armed women including female detectives, police officers, and soldiers, there is an overrepresentation of armed women who are White, thin, conventionally beautiful, and heterosexual. With a few notable exceptions, the fictional women detectives and police officers on the screen appear to struggle with balancing their femininity with their ability to routinely engage in lethal violence in ways not unlike the female soldiers.

In a comparative analysis of the media representations of three female soldiers of different racial and ethnic backgrounds who were captured and/or killed while on active duty, Joane Nagel and Lindsey Feitz concluded that "women appear to be more valuable media commodities than man where dramatic rescues are concerned. And as the treatment of the three women … indicates race also matters" (2007: 22).

Joane Nagel and Lindsey Feitz analyzed the media representations of three female soldiers of different racial backgrounds (Black, Native American, and White) and their analysis revealed that the female soldiers received dramatically different treatment by the media and the military. All three women were of similar rank. Their value as representational commodities varied by their race, maternal, and marital status with Jessica Lynch, the never-married young White blonde receiving the most media coverage as well as much larger financial compensation from the publishing industry, media, and the military. She was rewarded financially for being rescued.

Nagel and Feitz argued that the "Whiteness" and femininity of Jessica Lynch was used as a commodity by the U.S. military and the media. It had more value. In their words:

Not only Lynch's race, but her … sexual and moral worth were easy to market especially since her story reproduced familiar images from U.S. history and reflected longstanding popular media accounts … an updated version of seventeenth century captivity narratives which featured white women in peril, captured by savage Indians, rescued by heroic American men.

(2007: 34)

Jessica Lynch received national media coverage while the two other soldiers remained relatively invisible in the national media. Shoshana Johnson, a 31-year-old Black woman and the mother of one child, and Lori Piestewa, who was the first Native American women to die in combat, received little attention. Their representation contrasts

Table 4.2 Race, age, and maternal status of three U.S. soldiers killed or kidnapped in Iraq in comparative analysis.

Name	Home	Age	Race/Ethnicity	Marital Status	# of Children
Jessica Lynch	Palestine, West Virginia	19	White (blonde)	Unmarried	None
Shoshana Johnson	El Paso, Texas	31	Black	Single mother	1
Lori Piestewa	Tuba City, Arizona	23	Hopi Nation, Native American	Divorced	2

Source: Prepared by Melissa MacDonald.

sharply with that of Jessica Lynch whose staged rescue received the most media attention and the greatest financial rewards for being cast by the military in the role of a woman in need of rescue.

In contrast Shoshana Johnson, who was rescued with six male POWs during a routine search, received very little attention, no book deals, and a smaller pension than Lynch. Lori Piestewa, a member of the Hopi Nation and the divorced mother of two children, who was killed while delivering supplies, remains unknown to the general public and although a highway is named for her, she received little recognition in the national press. Nagel and Feitz argued that Jessica Lynch was:

> used as a propaganda tool and her femininity, rather than her identity as a soldier, was central to the representation of her as a female victim and a captive.... [She] was a "poster girl" for the US military and her rescue not only was planned and filmed, it was reenacted on network television as a dramatized spectacle of U.S. Special Operations ... she received a one million dollar advance on the first book published about her. Johnson has become neither a poster girl nor a millionaire; there was no instant book deal. A black or brown captive would have less market value and thus Shoshana Johnson was not chosen to stand in for the nation as a captive because as a black woman, a brunette, and a single mother, she lacked the "girl next door" appeal that the media valued in their rescue reports.
>
> (Nagel and Feitz 2007: 30)

In striking contrast to Jessica Lynch, the capture and rescue of Shoshana Johnson, a Black woman who was discovered in a routine search of houses in Nasiriyah, was not staged for media consumption.

> When compared to the media obsession with Jessica Lynch, she was barely noticed by the media. She remained relatively unknown to the public. Moreover, she did not receive the same level of compensation for her injuries.... Although both women have lingering physical problems from the incident and both have difficulty walking, the Army has classified Johnson as 30 percent disabled and Lynch as 80 percent disabled. This is a difference worth several hundred dollars more a month for Lynch.
>
> (Nagel and Feitz 2007: 45)

Nagel and Feitz concluded that:

> In their images and biographies we can see evidence of the military's reliance on and reproduction of class and race relations in the larger society: the recruitment of working class individuals for low-level, low-status, dangerous military work, the

valorization of whiteness and the devaluation of the contributions and sacrifices of soldiers of color.

(2007: 46)

In other words, the racial and class inequalities that exist in U.S. society are often reproduced in the U.S. Armed Services.

Lipstick Soldiers and Fashion Maneuvers

In her analysis of the ways that the U.S. military has managed the femininity of female soldiers, Cynthia Enloe notes that:

states have to expand more energy and resources in trying to shape their citizens' ideas about what constitutes an acceptable form of masculinity and an acceptable form of femininity than nonfeminist observers realize and than most state officials care to admit.

(2000: 236)

One way that the military managed the femininity and masculinity of its soldiers was through the design of female uniforms. This was an area where respectability, sexuality, and soldiering had to be coordinated. Fashion designers were hired and consulted. Cynthia Enloe argues that the military's investments in fashion design and the attention paid to the female uniform reflected the struggles by the military to attract potential recruits; uniforms needed at once to show that female soldiers could retain their femininity while also not making them appear too sexy and distinguishing them from male soldiers.

Figuring out which hat, which jacket, and which bra women should be officially issued as she entered into a masculinized, militarized enclave of the state, was thought necessary if that women's entry was to sustain a militarized version of national security, not subvert it. And this maneuver was difficult—and thus often confusing and even rather comical, at least to outsiders—precisely because militarizing women always has been pursued for the sake of controlling women in ways that maintain the sorts of masculinity that enhance militarism.

(Enloe 2000: 271)

Describing the fashion maneuvers, Enloe notes the centrality of femininity:

Preserving visible signs of women soldiers' femininity became a bureaucratic campaign, though one marked by contradictions. Army officers instructed a woman soldier to keep her hair short enough so that it reached just the collar of her uniform, but not so short as to appear "unfeminine." Women in the U.S. Marine Corps were required to tweeze their eyebrows in a regulation arch. An early 1980s army recruiting brochure suggests the military's ambivalence and institutional nervousness: below a color photo of a pretty woman smiling from under a camouflaged combat helmet is the caption "Some of our best soldiers wear lipstick."

(2000: 270)

Female veterans who have served as soldiers in Iraq and/or Afghanistan have described their experiences and struggles as they negotiated their sexuality while fulfilling their duties as professional soldiers in the company of their male peers. They describe their sexuality as both a resource and a liability as they were a magnet (or target) for the sexual desires of their male peers and often subjected to sexual harassment and/or sexual assault while serving in predominantly male platoons.

In a memoir by a female veteran titled *Love my Rifle More than You: Young and Female in the U.S. Army*, Kayla Williams, a 28-year-old White woman who served in Military Intelligence for five years in the United States and Iraq, describes the dilemmas that many female soldiers face because they are often hypersexualized by men in their platoons.

Sometimes, even now, I wake up before dawn and forget I am not a slut. The air is not quite dark, not quite light, and I lie absolutely still, trying to will myself to remember that this is *not* what I am ... I'm twenty-eight years old. Military intelligence, five years here and in Iraq. One of the 15 percent of the U.S. military that's female. And that whole 15 percent is trying to get past an old joke. "What's the difference between a bitch and a slut? A slut will fuck anyone, a bitch will fuck anyone but you." So if she's nice or friendly, outgoing or chatty—she's a slut. If she's distant, reserved or professional—she's a bitch.

(2005: 13)

Kayla Williams provides several insights into the paradoxes that female soldiers must manage. She argues that "Sex is key to any woman soldier's experience in the American military. No one likes to acknowledge it, but there's a strange sexual allure to being a woman and a soldier" (2005: 18). Describing how one particular female soldier provided blow jobs to every guy in her unit and that this had consequences for her and other female soldiers, she writes,

Making it tougher for the rest of us females to get our work done without having guys insinuate that blow jobs was part of our Advanced Individual Training.

It totally sucked, pun intended. It made it easy for guys over there to treat females as if we were less reliable. Which is enraging, since our skills as soldiers are what landed us in this war in the first place.

(2005: 18–19)

Although Williams' memoir of her experiences may not represent the experiences of all women in the Army, when they are analyzed alongside the Department of Defense reports on sexual assault, female veterans' reports of sexual trauma, and sociological surveys of female soldiers, she provides a personal portrait of a masculine occupational culture of the military that simultaneously empowers and disempowers female soldiers.

A woman soldier has to toughen herself up. Not just for the enemy, for battle, or for death. I mean toughen herself up to spend months awash in a sea of nervy, hyped-up guys who, when they're not thinking about getting killed, are thinking about getting laid. Their eyes on you all the time, your breasts, your ass—like there is nothing else to watch, no sun, no river, no desert, no mortar at night.

(2005: 13–14)

Describing her relationship with her gun, Kayla Williams writes:

I do love my M-4, the smell of it, of cleaning fluid, of gunpowder: the feeling of strength. The peacefulness on the firing range. I've come to look forward to that. It can

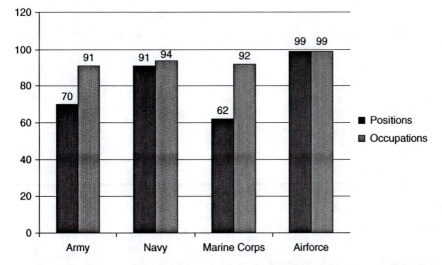

Figure 4.3 Percentage of military positions and occupations open to women, 2003.
Source: Population Reference Bureau, December 2004. Prepared by Melissa MacDonald.

turn you, though. Women are no different from men in their corruptibility. Women are just as competent—and just as incompetent.

(2005: 15)

Melissa Herbert, a sociologist who served in the enlisted ranks of the U.S. Army, conducted a study of how women in the military negotiate their gender and sexuality in an organizational setting in which although "masculinity is more valued than femininity, being perceived as masculine may have negative repercussions for women" (1998: 33). Herbert distributed surveys to women who had served in all four branches of the U.S. military and who had spent from 1 to 32 years on active duty. She also interviewed 14 women.

Based on her analysis of data from 285 completed surveys from 101 officers and 184 enlisted soldiers, including 73 who self-identified as lesbian or bisexual, she concluded that:

> Women also need to minimize their sexuality while still maintaining some degree of femininity. They must strike a balance between femininity and masculinity in which they are feminine enough to be perceived as women, specifically heterosexual women, yet masculine enough to be perceived as capable of soldiering.
>
> (Herbert 1988: 82)

In her analysis of the strategies employed by women to negotiate their gender and sexuality in the male-dominated world of the military, Herbert provides important insights into how women are:

> held accountable as women and as soldiers. Given that soldiering has been, and continues to be, constructed as a male pursuit, this dual accountability presents women with a conundrum of sorts. What kinds of actions, or strategies, do women employ to be accepted as women soldiers?
>
> (1988: 13)

Being perceived as "feminine" is something that has to be accomplished—it is a daily practice or what can be called a **gender display**. Drawing upon the concept of "Doing Gender" as conceptualized by Candace West and Sarah Fenstermaker, gender is best thought of as something that one "does," a performance, an achievement rather than a static state. First, one learns "gender rules" through socialization by parents, peers, teachers, authority figures. Herbert details the clothing strategies women reported in order to negotiate their femininity. She identified the following strategies:

- wearing make-up off duty (31 percent);
- wearing make-up on duty (38 percent);

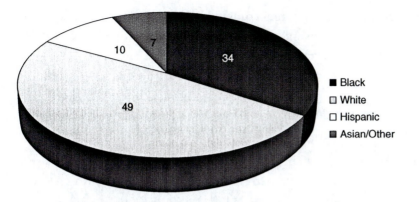

Figure 4.4 Percentage of female soldiers in U.S. Army by race/ethnicity.
Source: Population Reference Bureau, December 2004.

- wearing perfume or cologne (34 percent);
- wearing long hair (37 percent);
- wearing earrings in uniform (when permitted) (37 percent);
- wearing bright colors when off duty.

What we learn from the research of Herbert and others who have interviewed female veterans and active-duty soldiers is that women serving in the Armed Forces may feel the need to reject their femininity because, especially those in the most prestigious positions, their femininity is experienced as incompatible with being a soldier. Men do not have to negotiate contradictions between their masculinity and their status as soldiers because their masculinity is enhanced by their military service. The contradictions that women experience between their femininity and status as a soldier must be constantly negotiated and performed.

In a study of men and women in the Reserve Officers Training Corps (ROTC), Jennifer Silva interviewed 38 women and men. Silva found that:

women's transformative agency is limited by the cultural imperative of performing gender. Their identities as women are called into question in the military sphere.... Nearly all of the women in my sample ... find themselves unable to reconcile the contradictions between their identities as women and the qualities they deem necessary for combat or even a military career. In other words they see femininity as fundamentally incompatible with the core functions of the military but never call into question the importance and indeed centrality of femininity for themselves. On the contrary, these women view themselves as actively constructing meaningful identities that resist the hegemony of masculinity in the military. Yet, this focus on their individual choices obscures the cumulative effects of their actions: the reproduction of gender stratification and, ultimately, male privilege.

(2008: 954)

What can we learn from a different national context—one in which there is compulsory universal military service for men and women? Are the struggles around femininity different when the numbers are larger?

Israel and the United States: A Comparative Analysis of Militarized Femininity

The military industrial complex is the single largest employer in the United States and Israel. In both countries women have been barred from combat positions, which limits their promotion opportunities. In the United States, the policy of banning women from combat positions is changing. When compared with the United States, Israel could be perceived as having more potential gender equality in this arena because women are required to exercise the same "citizenship" rights as men in terms of defending the nation.

Israel has compulsory military service for men and women. In 1949, Israel passed the Security Service Law, which defined eligibility of compulsory service in universal terms and made no gender distinctions with regards to the roles that men and women could fill. Women, like men, are required to serve in the military although women serve fewer months. The difference in length of required service could be interpreted as a sign of gender inequality.

The United States and Israel share several important features including: 1) women are officially barred from most combat positions; 2) masculine organizational hierarchies; and 3) exclusion and marginalization of women from top leadership positions in the military. Military service in Israel, like the United States, has symbolic meaning as well as being evidence of citizenship.

The United States and Israel differ in several important ways including the fact that since 1973 the United States has an All-Volunteer Army while Israel has compulsory military service for men and women. Dafna Izraeli argues that:

> [military service] is equated with service to the Jewish collective and as such is constructed to be the basis for entitlement to full citizenship in the Jewish state. ... Married women are exempt from compulsory military service, but not from reserve service. Pregnant women and mothers are exempt from both the military and the reserve while fathers are not exempt. The law grants priority to women's family role over their obligations to military service. Since most women in Israel get married and have children, the law builds in the structure by which women are excluded from continued participation in the military, unless they choose the military as a career.
>
> (DeGroot and Peniston Bird 2000: 259, 261)

In an analysis of the Israeli Defense Force, Izraeli examines the **gender regimes** that structure it. A gender regime is an institutional arrangement that produces social inequalities in the positions that men and women occupy. Gender regimes are a feature of gendered institutions as theorized by Joan Acker. The underrepresentation of women in the top ranks of the U.S. Armed Services is a product of gender regimes.

In both the U.S. Armed Forces and the Israeli Defence Forces, the exclusion of women from combat roles is one of the ways that masculine privilege is reproduced. Combat experience is valued and is required in order to be promoted up the career ladder into most of the senior leadership positions. Describing women's subordination in the Israeli Defence Forces, Izraeli argues that:

> The exclusion of women from combat roles is the dominant mechanism for maintaining masculine privilege. In the security discourse, the combat experience is the unique tempering fire that turns a person (man) into a real soldier. Formal prerequisites for virtually all of the most senior positions and the majority of those below the senior levels include a period of service in the field. Thus, women are prevented from getting "experience in the field" and then their lack of experience becomes the justification for not promoting them to more senior positions.
>
> (2000: 263–64)

Thus, what we see in the case of Israel is that although women are "conscripted" and required to serve, their role as soldiers is subordinate to that of motherhood and, in contrast to men, they are given a number of ways to "opt out" including religious orthodoxy, marriage, pregnancy, and motherhood. Consequently the same polices that allow women to opt out of service are denied to their brothers, fathers, and husbands. These policies simultaneously privilege men as potential warriors while disadvantaging those men who would like to prioritize other roles such as that of being a father.

Who is a Combatant?: Gendered Boundaries and the Preservation of Male Supremacy

Between August 1990 and March 1991, the **Gulf War** was fought with the support of 40,000 women deployed to Saudi Arabia. Although American women represented only 7 percent of the total U.S. uniformed contingent, they were fighting in a war zone. Women were used differently from their male peers. In August 1990, the mainstream press reporters turned to Washington-based liberal women's organizations to construct their media images of the woman soldier.

Who qualifies for combatant status? Women are ineligible for (excluded from) combat positions solely due to their sex. This distinction is a **gendered boundary**.

Gendered boundaries are career obstacles that are implemented through policies that define some occupations and roles as "masculine." Combat has been defined as "masculine" and restricted to men. The official exclusion of women from combat positions reinforces gender ideologies. Gender ideologies are beliefs about what are appropriate and acceptable male and female roles. The idea that combat is an exclusively masculine activity and that heroism is reserved for men is a gender ideology that is enforced through specific military policies.

Scholars who have analyzed military policies and the actual experiences of women from memoirs by female soldiers have noted that the line between combatant and non-combatant is blurred in actual practice. In the words of Summerfield,

> In practice the distinction between combatant and non-combatant roles was hard to maintain because air attack, bombing and the threat of invasion dispersed the front line and brought it home. But the heroic status of the military civilian in wartime political rhetoric and popular culture polarized the two identities and increased the insecurity of the civilian.
>
> (2000: 119)

The exclusion of women from combat positions is a policy that perpetuates gender inequalities and sex segregation. In other words, gender segregation within the military is socially created and preserves male access to jobs that are higher in prestige (as evidenced by war medals). The exclusion of women from combat positions, or more precisely from the opportunity to engage in combat, is not merely symbolic. In addition to preventing women from acquiring experiences that are recognized and rewarded as heroism, which can lead to promotion to the top ranks. It also excludes women from achieving the highest pay grades, as well as from gaining the respect that they would if they are wounded in a combat zone while doing combat support duties. The command structure remains male dominated at the top precisely because women remain concentrated in those positions that do not allow them to have combat experience in the command structure. Combat experience enables one to become eligible for promotions that can lead to higher.

Men continue to occupy the vast majority of leadership positions in the Armed Forces and the military remains a highly masculinized institution. The military also differs from the civilian labor force in a number of significant ways. First, its age structure is significantly younger. "More than half of the enlisted women in the armed forces are below age 25, as are almost half of the enlisted men. In the civilian labor force, men and women below age 25 make up only 15 percent of the labor force, in contrast to 50 percent" (*Population Bulletin* 2004).

DISCUSSION QUESTIONS

1. Why is "femininity" experienced as being incompatible with being a soldier? Explain what this means. Identify and discuss three strategies employed by female soldiers to display their femininity while also fulfilling their duties as soldiers.

2. In her memoir Kayla Williams identifies and discusses the "paradoxes" of being a female soldier. Read a memoir by a female veteran. Identify and describe at least one paradox that they experience as a soldier and as a woman.

3. Go online and read several news stories from militarytimes.com. Based on your analysis discuss the issue of gender equity. How does the *Military Times* report on gender equity issues for soldiers?

4. What is a gender regime? How does the military's gender regime in Israel differ from that of the U.S. Armed Forces? Discuss the differences that are produced by these regimes in terms of the experiences and expectations of female and male soldiers?

5. Select a profile of a female soldier from a magazine, documentary film, or a television show that profiles or represents active-duty female soldiers. How do they manage and conceptualize their femininity? How do they negotiate masculinity and gendered violence? Do they perceive it as a routine and relatively mundane part of their job? How do they describe their training and skill with weapons? Do they see their roles as mothers, daughters, wives, and women as being in conflict with their jobs as professional soldiers? Draw on their specific analyses of their situation.

V: The Economics of Military Motherhood

～～×～～

You are a single mother. You have two children including one under the age of six. What is the best job situation for you? It might be picking up arms and joining the military. If you don't live in France, state-subsidized childcare, healthcare, prenatal care, and after-school programs may not be affordable.

American mothers, whether they are single, married, divorced, or widowed and currently serving in the U.S. Armed Services, can expect to receive "family" benefits that are unmatched in many jobs in the civilian labor force. The U.S. Armed Forces has transformed itself into one of the most family-friendly pro-family institutions in the United States. For example, soldiers receive free or subsidized housing, healthcare, pensions, education, childcare, and other benefits that would be very expensive, barely affordable, and unavailable to their poor, working-class, or lower-middle-class peers in the United States. It turns out that bearing arms for the federal government is one of the better-paying job options for young women from impoverished families, working-class backgrounds, or immigrants seeking employment and/or an expedited track to citizenship.

In addition to salary, the family and medical benefits available to members of the Armed Forces are more generous than those available to many workers in the civilian labor force who have comparable levels of education. This is an incentive to the parents of children and particularly to single, divorced, or widowed mothers and fathers.

On September 30, 2010 there were 213,823 women serving on active duty in the U.S. Armed Forces. Women represent 13.5 percent of the Army, 7.5 percent of the Marine Corps, 16.0 percent of the Navy, and 19.2 percent of the Air Force. Women compose 14.6 percent of the employees of the Department of Defense. A comparative analysis of the wages of women serving in the Armed Forces and women working in the civilian labor force can illuminate the relationship between gender and occupational segregation and the economic benefits (and social costs) to women of working in predominantly male occupations.

Women enter the Armed Forces for a number of reasons. However, for single mothers, married mothers, or divorced mothers, there are a number of economic incentives and family benefits that make the military a desirable workplace for women, particularly those without a college education. First, for women who are Black, Native American, or Latinas, the military is perceived as a less discriminatory workplace.

Table 5.1 My Army benefits.

Military Social Welfare	Compensation
Subsidized Housing	The Basic Allowance for Housing (BAH) offsets the cost of housing when soldiers live off base. BAH rates are based on location, rank, and family status. BAH is the second-largest piece of compensation for most soldiers.
Healthcare	Soldiers are automatically covered by a comprehensive HMO-type healthcare plan called TRICARE that provides medical and dental care at little or no cost.
Subsidized Food	The Basic Allowance for Subsistence (BAS) is used to pay for food for enlisted soldiers and officers authorized to eat off base. Most soldiers who qualify for BAS receive more than $200 per month.
Education	The Post-9/11 GI Bill provides up to 36 months of benefits for education at an institution of higher learning. Benefits of the program include tuition fees, a monthly living allowance, books and supplies. Benefits can also be transferred to a spouse or dependent children.
Subsidized Childcare	Army Child and Youth Services (CYS) provide affordable childcare programs for Army families. Costs are typically based on rank and pay grade (i.e. child development centers provide full-daycare, part-daycare, and hourly care for children 6 weeks to 5 years of age.)

Source: myarmybenefits.us.military.org. Prepared by Melissa MacDonald.

Despite the gains of the civil rights movement, there continue to be informal practices that discriminate against Blacks and Latinos. Second, the U.S. labor market provides very limited job options for high-school graduates who cannot afford a college education and are members of impoverished families. In a different labor market that provided them with a wider range of occupational choices, these women might be less willing to work for an institution that requires them to engage in dangerous work, undergo weapons training, and to participate in state-sanctioned violence.

The brutal economic realities for young women from working-class backgrounds whose families cannot afford college without federal support and cannot afford to support their adult children is that the military may be one of the best options available to them since they do not have the resources to pay for college and the luxury of spending years working in unpaid internships to secure professional jobs.

The military, an organization that trains women and men to kill, may also offer a more pro-family environment than most civilian jobs in the United States. For single mothers and single fathers raising children this is not an insignificant resource. In contrast to the civilian workforce who must struggle to find adequate and affordable childcare, the military offers excellent compensation packages to families that one could argue make it one of the more "socialist" institutions in the United States. If we consider the healthcare plans, subsidized food, free or subsidized housing, and other programs, it is a much better deal than most civilians can hope for in the United States. In contrast to European countries like France, working-class and middle-class families in the United States do not have access to affordable childcare, adequate healthcare, or even subsidized housing. Describing the attractive financial packages that the Armed Services established after it became an All-Volunteer Army, Linda Bird Francke writes:

> The family benefits made the services a particular mecca for single parents: in 1989 there were proportionately twice as many single parents in the Navy as in the civilian population. Unlike their civilian counterparts, single parents in the military received free prenatal, obstetrical and pediatric care along with a plethora of other support systems including subsidized child care, schooling, housing and dependents allowances. Their children benefited as well. Service children could join on-base youth, summer, after-school and summer job programs as "baggers" in based commissaries, and church retreats.
>
> (1997: 139)

In the United States, if we compare U.S. civilian women to military women, we see that although civilian women may have more flexibility in terms of the exact hours they work and to some extent their work conditions, they do not have access to the same subsidies and thus would have to earn much more than their military peers in order to purchase the services that are provided as part of their compensation package.

DISCUSSION QUESTIONS

1. Go to the U.S. Department of Labor website and review occupational categories by pay and benefits. Identify and describe five occupations that pay comparable wages to the lowest ranks of enlisted personnel in the U.S. Army. Compare the pay to the salary scale of civilian women to women who are enlisted members of the Army. How do they compare in terms of salary, work conditions, and benefits?

2. You are the single mother of two children and you are notified that your job is being discontinued. There are very few jobs in your community. You begin to do research on the available state and federal benefits for an unemployed single parent of children in your community (city, state) because you may need assistance. Your sister is employed in the U.S. Army and has been on active duty for three years. Calculate the cost of living for a family of three or four and now calculate the benefits that this same family would receive if the mother was employed in the Army, Navy, or Air Force. Compare and contrast the military as a welfare institution to government welfare benefits available today. What is the maximum amount and form of support (food stamps, TANF (Temporary Aid to Needy Families), and housing vouchers?)

3. For some, the increase in the numbers of female soldiers has been interpreted as evidence of increased gender equality and as a symbol of feminist empowerment. Yet they are also feminized and subordinated within a masculine and historically

all-male institution. They remain a numerical minority. In what ways are female soldiers simultaneously empowered and disempowered?

4. What policy changes do you think are needed to transform the military into a more gender-egalitarian institution? Identify two specific policy changes that you would recommend in order to counter negative gender stereotypes about women as soldiers.

VI: Double Jeopardy

Female Soldiers in the Military–Sexual Complex

>≈≈✕≈≈

On December 14, 2007 Maria Lauterbach, a Marine, who was eight months pregnant, disappeared from a Marine Corps Base Camp in North Carolina. The burned remains of her body were found in a fire pit in the backyard of Cesar Armando Laurean, another Marine, who worked closely with her as a supervisor. Laurean, a married 21-year-old native of Mexico, fled to Mexico after her disappearance. This case became a national sensation. On April 5, 2008 her murder was featured on *America's Most Wanted*. Five days later Corporal Cesar Laurean was apprehended in Mexico. He was court martialed and found guilty of first-degree murder and currently serves a life sentence. The failure of the Marines to respond effectively to the **rape** complaint of Maria Lauterbach and her subsequent murder called attention to a problematic and dangerous institutional culture which failed to protect female recruits, trainees, and soldiers from rape and aggravated sexual assault by fellow soldiers.

According to an article on October 28 posted in the *Military Times* the Marines did not properly investigate Lauterbach's complaints of sexual assault and did not sufficiently protect the 20 year old from Laurean, a co-worker who raped her. An investigation into her case generated a highly critical report of the Marines. Emery P. Dalesio, reporting for the *Military Times*, wrote:

> The report found that the details of Lauterbach's rape complaint were not entered into a database maintained by the bases' Sexual Assault and Prevention Response Programs for 6 months after they were reported. NCIS agents never interviewed some potential witnesses after Lauterbach's allegations and others were not interviewed until months later.
>
> (Dalesio 2011)

On March 7, 2007 Salon.com published an investigative report on military sexual assault titled "The Private War of Women Soldiers" by Helen Benedict. This story inspired *The Invisible War*, a documentary by Kirby Dirk and Amy Ziering, which was shown across the United States in the summer of 2012 and won the 2012 Audience Award at the Sundance Film Festival. This film presents testimonies by female veterans that echo the lawsuit filed in 2012 against the Department of Defense (the Pentagon).

It was inspired by the personal testimonies of military sexual survivors (rape victims) who shared their stories with journalists (Benedict, 2007, 2009), as well as Department of Defense reports that reveal the military is not a safe place for active-duty female soldiers. *The Invisible War* examines the epidemic of military rape and shows how the Department of Defense has mishandled rape cases by not providing appropriate channels for reporting these assaults that were outside of the "chain of command." The viewer learns that female soldiers who report their rape may face punishment, ostracism, and eventually be forced out of their careers, instead of being offered emotional, psychological, or other forms of support.

Among the rape survivors presented in the documentary is Ariana Klay, a former Marine Corps officer, who was gang raped by a senior officer and his civilian friend while she was stationed at the elite Marine Barracks in Washington, D.C. A veteran of Iraq, she was driven out of the Marines after the rape. Klay is one of the eight current and former members of the U.S. military who alleged in a federal lawsuit filed in 2012 that they were raped, assaulted, or harassed during their service and suffered retaliation when they reported it to their superiors.

In April 2012 *The Invisible War* was screened to Leon Panetta, Secretary of Defense, and other leaders in the Defense Department, several months before its June release. Shortly after its release Panetta announced sweeping changes to military policy and to the Uniform Code of Military Justice, which are intended to address the systematic abuses and inconsistent handling of the reporting, processing, and prosecution of sexual assault complaints and cases.

When women enter the Marines to become trained to serve their country, they are entering an institutional space that places women at increased risk (when compared with their civilian peers) of rape and repeated aggravated sexual assault and at high risk of particular forms of assault such as "**command rape**." Although women have some agency, female trainees who enter the Armed Services at the lowest ranks are constrained because they have virtually no freedom of movement or control over their work conditions. They have not yet earned "privileges" and thus are very vulnerable when relating to men (and women) of senior rank. They cannot necessarily transfer to a different unit if they are abused. They must often endure sexual abuse in order to maintain social "cohesion" within their units. At the same time, the Armed Services offer them training, resources, and other forms of material support that civilian women from poor families have difficulty accessing in a declining and class-stratified economy.

In 2007 the Veterans' Administration opened a new treatment facility in New Jersey specifically for female veterans. This is the only residential treatment facility for women veterans in the United States to treat women for **military sexual trauma** (MST). Prior to 2005 military women did not have the option of receiving treatment after sexual assault unless they revealed the identity of their assailant. According to the Veterans' National Center for Posttraumatic Stress Disorder, 15 percent of veterans who had served in Iraq and/or Afghanistan reported a history of sexual assault or harassment.

Many military women are reluctant to report sexual assault because it typically involves men with whom they work closely or their male superiors or commanders. There has been a lack of confidentiality because there was not a separate reporting channel for handling sexual assault investigations. Women feared that they would be punished, and not advance in their military career if they reported their abuse or refused to continue working under the command of someone who had sexually assaulted them.

In a sociological review of the literature on female veterans who have served in Iraq and Afghanistan, Joanne Nagel and Lindsey Feitz write:

> We find that the US military-sexual complex has incorporated and exploited women and femininity to achieve combat goals, and we conclude that, despite much official rhetoric about the limitations of women in combat, the deployment of women as weapons of war has been integrated into the US military's structure and operations.
>
> (Feitz and Nagel 2007: 20–21)

Writing for *Newsweek* and reporting on military rape, in an interview conducted in November 2007 David Botti writes that:

> Sexual assault is about power. Someone who already has authority over someone can use that as a way to be sexually inappropriate with them. From the very beginning military personnel are trained to follow orders, and so they're at a disadvantage; it's harder for them to say no to somebody. In one case this sergeant ordered a woman to come to his barracks after lights-out.... She didn't really think of it as an illegal order, and then once he got her there, he sexually assaulted her.
>
> (2007)

In March 2010 the Department of Defense released its annual report. This report revealed that there has been a significant increase in reported sexual assaults in the military "including a 16 percent increase in reported assaults occurring in combat areas, principally Iraq and Afghanistan." According to the Department of Defense more than half of these assaults, 53 percent:

> were assaults by service members on other service members ... In Iraq, women still only make up one in ten troops, and because they are not evenly distributed, they often serve in a platoon with few other women or none at all. This isolation, along with the military's traditional and deep-seated hostility toward women, can cause problems that many female soldiers find as hard to cope with as war itself: degradation and sexual persecution by their comrades, and

loneliness instead of the camaraderie that every soldier depends on for comfort and survival.

(Bulmiller 2010)

According to the Pentagon sexual assaults are underreported by female veterans and constitute a serious problem for the U.S. military, which is increasingly dependent upon women soldiers who are now serving in combat areas. In 2011 the Government Accountability Office (GAO) delivered a report to the House Veterans' Affairs Committee which found that:

sexual assaults were underreported and, when they were reported, ... officials often did not follow up through designated channels. For instance, V.A. policy requires that accusations of rape be reported to the department's Office of the Inspector Generals. Yet the report, based on a three-year investigation at five facilities, found that nearly two-thirds of the 67 rape accusations never made it to the office.

(Botti 2008)

Until 2012, the Armed Services were not required to maintain documentary evidence collected on sexual assault investigations. And this evidence, including that from rape kits or medical kits, could be routinely destroyed. There has been inconsistent record keeping across the services and the lack of a database to collect records.

On March 8, 2010 *Time* published a story on the sexual assaults of female soldiers. This report was based on Pentagon reports which revealed that rape and sexual assault were not uncommon and that a rape culture pervades the military.

The Pentagon's latest figures show that nearly 3,000 women were sexually assaulted in fiscal year 2008, up 9% from the year before; among women serving in Iraq and Afghanistan, the number rose 25%. When you look at the entire universe of female veterans, close to a third say they were victims of rape or assault while they were serving—twice the rate of the civilian population. The problem is even worse than that. The Pentagon estimates that 80% to 90% of sexual assaults go unreported, and it's no wonder. Anonymity is all but impossible....

(Gibbs 2010)

In contrast to their male peers, female soldiers are typically exposed to much higher levels of sexual assault, sexual harassment, and abuse compared to their civilian peers. This is particularly the case when they are a numerical minority in their platoon.

Staff Sergeant Cassandra Cantu, a six-year veteran of the U.S. Air Force, describes her experiences in Afghanistan:

> While I was there, I was sexually harassed daily. I lived in constant fear for my life doing convoys and feared being raped when I returned to base. I felt the eyes of the men on me all the time.
>
> (Benedict 2009: 81)

Another veteran of the Iraq War, Eli Painted Crow, the grandmother of seven, described her experiences of being routinely raped and the lack of support from male superiors:

> Sexual assault happened to me several times in my twenty-two years in the military, a couple of times that succeeded. I got even with them in my own way, but I never reported them because nobody believes you.
>
> (Benedict 2009: 79)

Drawing upon interviews with 40 women who had served in the Iraq War and in Afghanistan, Helen Benedict describes the social isolation and the conditions that female soldiers reported.

> "I was the only female in my platoon of fifty to sixty men," said army specialist Chantelle Henneberry, a Montanan who served in Iraq from 2005 to 2006 with the 172nd Stryker Brigade out of Alaska. "My company consisted of fifteen hundred men—marines, navy, air force and army and under eighteen women. I was fresh meat to hungry men. The mortar rounds that came in daily did less damage to me than the men with whom I shared my food.... The prevailing attitude in the military from women, as well as men, is to regard a woman who reports sexual assault as a traitor, a weakling, a slut, or a liar, and soldiers often punish such women by ostracizing her; turning their backs when she walks into a room or refusing to speak or listen to her."
>
> (2009: 81)

In December of 2010 the American Civil Liberties Union (ACLU) sued the Department of Defense for access to their rape records. According to an article by John Christoffersen in the *Military Times*:

> "The government's refusal to even take the first step in providing comprehensive and accurate information about the sexual trauma inflicted upon our women and man in uniform ... is all too telling," said Anuradha Bhagwait, a former Marine Captain and executive director of SWAN (Service Women's Action Network).

"The government prosecutes 8 percent of military sex offenders, while 40 percent of civilian sex offenders are prosecuted, according to the lawsuit."

(Christoffersen December 13, 2010)

One consequence of the mishandling of sexual trauma cases by the Department of Defense is that women and men who have been diagnosed with Posttraumatic Stress Disorder (PTSD) are also sexual trauma victims, yet they are often not able to provide sufficient "evidence" due to the fact that they were assaulted by commanding officers or members of their platoon, and these matters, until recently, were handled internally. There was too much discretion granted to supervising officers. Since 2010 there have been changes to this policy as more attention has been given to this issue.

Female Veterans and Sexual Trauma

Between October 2001 and October 2007, 125,000 veterans received medical care at Veterans' Administration facilities. In the first study of its kind and the largest survey of veterans, "almost one out of seven female veterans of Afghanistan or Iraq who visit a Veterans Affairs center for medical care report being a victim of sexual assault or harassment during military duty" (Botti 2008). A separate study by the Pentagon argues that sexual assault is severely underreported and that as many of 80–90 percent of the victims do not report it for fear of ostracism.

Annual reports from the Department of Defense (the Pentagon), memoirs, surveys of female veterans, and journalistic accounts all reveal that the sexual assaults and sexual abuse of female soldiers while on active duty in the Armed Forces are routine. Female soldiers serving in the U.S. Armed Forces are exposed to more sexual assaults than their civilian counterparts. Thus, if women who are trained in handling weapons are not able to protect themselves from their male peers in the military, why would civilian women be more likely to be able to protect themselves from intimate partner violence or domestic violence? The U.S. military, like civilian society, remains male-dominated and women continue to be treated like sexual commodities and/or prey by a segment of their male comrades. The rape culture that exists outside of the military does not end when women enlist.

Moral Waivers

Due to a shortage of volunteer recruits, criminal records are no longer a barrier to entry into the Armed Services.

Since 9/11 the military has been applying "moral waivers" to recruits, which means taking people with criminal records, something the Defense Department once abhorred. Rules on waivers vary with different branches of the military, but over 125,000 recruits with criminal histories enlisted between 2004 and 2007, including those with records in aggravated assault. For example, according to Benedict "The use of moral waivers has risen 42 percent since the year 2000.... In 2006, more than 1 in 10 army recruits had criminal histories."

(Benedict 2009: 88)

News reports in the mainstream media often included the voices of women who reported that they were afraid to report military sexual assault because of their fear of being punished or ostracized. If we compare female soldiers who were assaulted by their commanding officers, a senior officer, or a fellow soldier to civilian women who are assaulted, we find that female soldiers, who are trained in weapons' use, appear to be at a higher risk of sexual assault because of the masculine occupational culture and the conditions under which they work compared with their civilian peers. Like their civilian sisters, they may also be raped by an intimate—a member of their platoon, their commanding officer, or someone they know. Also when we consider women who are assaulted by their commanding officers, or their husbands, lovers, domestic partners or relatives, possessing a gun may not empower them.

Women who serve in the Armed Forces are trained in weapons use, and authorized to use lethal force and to kill in order to resolve national and international conflicts. The conditions under which they operate a gun (economic, emotional, physical, legal) differ greatly from those of women who arm themselves as civilian mothers, wives, or as single women without the support of a military–industrial complex. Women who arm themselves to protect themselves and their families must have the resources to purchase guns, enroll in classes, learn how to properly use them and they do so within a complex set of state, federal, and local laws. Women who use guns for recreational use in hunting and target shooting must also provide their own weapons, and learn to use them properly.

The high rate of sexual trauma reported by female veterans demonstrates that women serving in the Armed Forces, that is women who are trained to use arms effectively, are not able to defend themselves from gendered violence while on active duty. In fact, they may be at higher risk of sexual assault than their female civilian peers due to the masculinist rape culture in the U.S. military. Women are not only a numerical minority in the Armed Services but, more importantly, they remain underrepresented in the leadership ranks, which has limited their ability to transform or challenge the masculinist culture of the military.

DISCUSSION QUESTIONS

1. Identify and discuss two policies that the U.S. Armed Forces could implement to reduce the risk of sexual assault for female soldiers serving in predominantly

male platoons. Explain how and why you think these polices would decrease the incidence of sexual assault.

2. Read a memoir written by a female veteran or listen to an interview (podcast) of an interview with a female veteran. How does she describe her struggles as a soldier? Does she identify sexual harassment or sexual assault as a primary issue? How did she negotiate her femininity and sexuality?

3. Watch *The Invisible War*, a 2012 documentary film by Kirby Dick that won the Audience Award at the Sundance Film Festival. It lasts 97 minutes. After watching this film, answer the following questions. How were your stereotypes or preconceptions about the lives of female soldiers altered by this film? What did you learn that surprised you most about the emotional consequences of violence and the response to violence in the U.S. Armed Forces?

4. How do racial inequality and class inequality shape the media representations of armed women in mainstream culture? In other words, what differences do you see in the media portrayals of White women compared with Black, Latina, Native American, and/or Asian women who are armed? Give specific examples from television news, films, and magazines.

VII: Conclusion

Gender Equality in the U.S. Armed Forces

I n 1972 Title VII of the 1964 Civil Rights Act mandated gender equality. Prior to 1972 women had very restricted roles in the military and in police departments. They did not have the same titles or positions as their male colleagues. They earned less and they did not hold leadership positions. They were also barred from competing for promotion on the same basis as men. One measure of gender (in)equality has been the belief that women needed to be protected from violence because they were more fragile.

The presence of women has not radically changed the leadership structure of the U.S. Armed Services, in part because women remain underrepresented in the senior ranks of all five branches of the Armed Services. Their absence has had serious consequences for women who have been sexually assaulted because there are few, if any, senior women to whom they can turn for support in these situations. In most of the senior ranks of the U.S. Armed Services the men holding the highest positions are "combat veterans," that is, they have served in positions that were officially defined as "combat" positions rather than "support" positions.

A number of recent policy changes recent to the Uniform Military Code of Justice could help transform the masculine "rape" cultural in the Armed Services. Prior to 2012 it was almost impossible for many victims of sexual assault to prove that they had been assaulted due to the lack of evidence, the destruction of evidence, the lack of eyewitnesses, the rank and status of the sexual offender who might be a commanding officer, and the general lack of motivation on the part of the male leadership to prosecute cases. Whether women were assaulted during their first weeks of training by a male instructor, or whether they were gang-raped after having served many years, there were institutional barriers to their reports of sexual assault being handled properly and taken seriously. In the words of Representative Chellie Pingree, a Democrat from Maine, who introduced a bill into Congress that would make it easier for female veterans who are survivors of sexual assault to receive compensation for military sexual trauma, "It's very difficult to prove sexual assault in the current system, which makes it just as difficult for veterans who have been victims to qualify for the treatments and benefits that they need to recover" (Maze 2011).

On April 16, 2012, Leon Panetta, the Secretary of Defense, held a press conference in which he announced the establishment of **Special Victims Units** (SVUs) in each branch or service. These SVUs will be authorized to establish procedures to not only investigate and prosecute rape and sexual assault cases but also to develop profiles and learn how sexual predators operate so that they can prevent assaults and reduce the number of cases. There will also be a central database that will act as a depository for the collection and permanent storage of cases from all five branches of the U.S. Armed Services. Major policy changes to the Uniform Code of Military Justice are a rare occurrence. This is evidence that the U.S. Armed Forces is finally starting to take seriously the trauma that it has inflicted on its own soldiers.

A number of problems have made it difficult for rape victims to report their crimes, and then to have the offenders prosecuted. These include: 1) the routine destruction of evidence including rape kits and medical kits; 2) the discretion of the commanding officer who was not required to send files for investigation; 3) the lack of confidentiality for victims reporting crimes committed by members of their unit; 4) fear of retaliation or ostracism and in some cases more violence; and 5) dismissal on "false" charges as a form of punishment.

The U.S. Armed Forces has begun to establish systematic policies to handle sexual assault and to make the military more accommodating to the needs of female veterans. It is still too early to know how the the rape culture in the military will change and whether being "feminine" or female will continue to be a liability for sexually active women.

Being armed and knowing how to effectively use guns does not appear to guarantee women sufficient protection from gendered violence. Government statistics which acknowledge that female soldiers underreport sexual assault, combined with personal testimonies, memoirs, journalist reports, and sociological analyses all reveal that being trained in firearms does not protect women from intimate partner violence or from sexual assault by fellow soldiers (or other workplace intimates). Women who arm themselves to serve their country should expect to be protected from gendered violence among their peers. We have learned that armed soldiers appear to be at high risk of aggravated sexual assault and rape because, until recently, there was minimal, if any, fear among male offenders that they would be held accountable or prosecuted. The culture of rape that exists in the civilian world appears to become exaggerated and heightened in the military sphere where there is a strict hierarchy and there are few women at the top of the chain of command.

Gender Segregation in Combat Units

Gender segregation in the workplace has been a stable feature of the U.S. job market and something that feminists have fought to eliminate. Feminists have argued that excluding women from participating in all job categories (even dangerous ones) in the U.S. Armed Forces is discriminatory and reinforces gender-segregated occupations for women within the military.

Feminists have argued (and non-feminists in the U.S. Armed Services acknowledge) that barring women from receiving training in "combat" battalions restricts their opportunities for promotion and advancement to the highest leadership ranks. In other words, Pentagon policies that have barred women from applying for positions in infantry and direct combat units are a gendered barrier, a form of **gender segregation**, and an obstacle created by institutional policies that creates systematic discrimination against women in terms of promotion into the leadership ranks. Within the military women become an inferior "class" because they have restricted opportunities for promotions that are rewarded on the basis of combat experience. Even if they are exposed to violence and severely wounded in the same attack as male combatants they are typically not eligible for certain honors because they were not "classified" as combats and the way that they acquired their wounds is not defined as honorable.

On April 18, 2012, the Marine Corps announced that the **Marine Corps Infantry Training Battalions School** in Quantico, Virginia will enroll its first-ever female students. The Infantry Training Battalion School trains marines who will be eligible to serve as combat officers. The Marine Corps, which has been viewed as one of the most "traditionalist" of the Armed Services, recently made a major policy change that will remove discriminatory barriers to women who want to acquire combat experience. In an article titled "USMC-4-Star: Women to Attend Infantry School" published in the *Marine Corps Times*, the reader learns that:

> This past winter, the Defense Department published a report saying that nonlinear combat against a shadowy enemy in Iraq and Afghanistan has negated the notion of a frontline behind which women can be kept safe. Working in support roles, 144 women have been killed in action and 865 injured since the invasions of Afghanistan and Iraq, according to the Defense Department data.
>
> (*Marine Corps Times* 2012)

The Department of Defense now recognizes that the prohibitions against women serving in combat zones is not logical and makes no sense in Iraq and Afghanistan where there is no "front line" and thus no safe zones for women and men serving in "support" roles as mechanics, cooks, or delivering supplies.

Women who bear arms for the state should also be protected from gendered violence from their fellow soldiers while on active duty. Female soldiers serving in the U.S. Armed Services appear to be at higher risk of sexual assault and other forms of violence when compared with their unarmed and untrained civilian peers. In the aftermath of the 2007 murder of Maria Lauterbach and the establishment of SUVs to track, monitor, and prosecute sexual assault cases, another sex scandal rocked the U.S. Armed Forces.

Under the leadership of Leon Panetta, the U.S. Armed Forces began to implement policies in 2012 designed to support the victims of military sexual assault. The new

SUVs may not be enough to really transform the "masculine" culture of rape, which is a pervasive condition of employment for soldiers. Although the documentary *The Invisible War* has increased the civilian population's awareness of military sexual assault and of the sexual trauma that female veterans must manage, the rape culture in the U.S. Armed Services parallels the same culture in civilian society.

In what was described as "a sweeping sex scandal" at the Lackland-San Antonio Air Force Base, six instructors were charged with rape and adultery. At Lackland the 35,000 Air Force recruits who graduate each year are trained by a group of 475 predominantly (90%) male instructors. Approximately one in five recruits are female. Writing for *The Army Times*, an online military news site, Weissert reported on a trial that concluded in July of 2012:

> A military jury found Staff Sgt. Luis Walker guilty Friday night on all 28 charges he faced, including rape, aggravated sexual conduct and multiple counts of aggravated sexual assault [...] Walker is among 12 Lackland instructors investigated for sexual misconduct towards at least 31 female trainees. Six instructors have been charged from rape to adultery. Walker is the first to stand trial.
>
> (Weissert 2012)

During the past four decades, women have greatly increased their participation in state violence as "active-duty" soldiers. However, recurring sex scandals demonstrate that a masculine culture of sexual violence exists in the U.S. Armed Services—one in which female soldiers are often sexual prey.

DISCUSSION QUESTIONS

1. Do an internet search on online magazines and newspapers that target women and men serving in the Armed Forces. Read ten issues of a paper like *Marine Corps Times* or other military papers published between 1990 and 2010. How are female soldiers represented?

2. Select one branch of the Armed Services (Air Force, Army, Navy, Marines, Coast Guard). Then research what percentage of enlisted service members in this branch are women. What percentage of the leadership (highest ranks) are female? What is their average age? In what jobs are they concentrated? Do you think that the job opportunities available to female soldiers are a reliable measure of gender equality in the Armed Services?

Bibliography

Abron, JoNina M. 1998. "Serving the People: The Survival Programs of the Black Panther Party." Pp. 157–76 in *The Black Panther Party Revisited*, ed. Charles E. Jones, Baltimore. MD: Black Classic Press.

Joan Acker. 1990. "Hierarchies, Jobs, Bodies: A Theory of Gendered Organizations." *Gender and Society* 4(2): 139–58.

———. 1992. "Gendered Institutions." *Contemporary Sociology 21*: 565–69.

Alter, Jonathan. 1999. "On the Cusp of a Crusade." *Newsweek* (May 10): 59.

Anderson, Jack. 1966. "Should We Send Our Women Soldiers to Vietnam?" *The Washington Post* (January 2).

Bassin, Alana. 1997. "Why Packing a Pistol Perpetuates Patriarchy." *Hastings Women's Law Journal 8*(2) (Fall): 351–63.

Benedict, Helen. 2007. "The Private War of Women Soldiers." *Salon.com*, first posted on March 7, 2007: 04:42 AM. PST.

———. 2009. *The Lonely Soldier: The Private War of Women Serving in Iraq*. Boston, MA: Beacon Press.

Berger, Dan. 2006. *Outlaws of America: The Weather Underground and the Politics of Solidarity*. Edinburgh: AK Press.

Blair, M. Elizabeth, and Eva M. Hyatt. 1995. "The Marketing of Guns to Women: Factors Influencing Gun-Related Attitudes and Gun Ownership by Women." *Journal of Public Policy & Marketing* 14(1) (Spring): 117–27.

Blauner, Robert. 1972. *Racial Oppression in America*. New York: Harper Collins.

Blodgett-Ford, Sayoko. 1993. "Do Battered Women Have a Right to Bear Arms?" *Yale Law and Policy Review 11*: 509–57.

Botti, David. 2007. "Sexual Assault in the Ranks." *Newsweek* (November 5). Retrieved September 15, 2011 (http://www.thedailybeast.com/newsweek/blogs/soldiers-home/2007/11/05/sexual-assault-in-the-ranks.html).

———. 2008. "15 Percent of Veterans Report Sexual Trauma to the VA." *Newsweek* (October 28).

Browder, Laura. 2006. *Her Best Shot: Women and Guns in America*. Chapel Hill: University of North Carolina Press.

Brown, Elaine. 1992. *A Taste of Power: A Black Woman's Story*. New York/London: Doubleday.

Bulmiller, Elisabeth. 2010. "Sex Assault Reports Rise in Military." *New York Times* (Late edition/East Coast) (March 17): A14.

Carroll, Joseph. 2005. "Gun Ownership and Use in America." Gallup poll (November 22).

Christoffersen, John. 2010. "ACLU Sues for Release of Military Rape Records." Retrieved December 13, 2010 (http://www.militarytimes.com/news/2010/12/ap-aclu-military-rape-lawsuit-121310w).

Cohen, Sandy. 2012. "Documentary Investigates Rape in the Military." Retrieved January 25, 2012 (http://www.marinecorpstimes/news/2012/01/ap-documentary-examines-rape-in-the-military-012512).

Dalesio, Emery P. 2011. "IG Report Criticizes Lejeune in Lauterbach case." Posted October 28, 2011 (http://www.marinecorpstimes.com/news/2011/10/ap-marine-lejeune-inspector-general-report-criticizes-102811).

D'Amico, Francine, and Laurie Weinstein. 1999. *Gender Camouflage: Women and the US Military*. New York/London: New York University Press.

Dees-Thomases, Donna and Alison Hendrie. 2004. *Looking for a Few Good Moms: How One Mother Rallied A Million Others Against the Gun Lobby*. New York: Rodale Books.

DeGroot, Gerard J., and Corinna Peniston Bird. 2000. *A Soldier and A Woman: Sexual Integration in the Military*. Harlow, U.K.: Longman.

Deputy Chief of Staff ARMY G-1. 2010. "Demographics—Army G-1 Human Resources." *Deputy Chief of Staff ARMY G-1—Home Page* (Mar. 23). Retrieved June 1, 2011 (http://www.armyg1.army.mil/hr/demographics.asp).

Dizard, Jon. 2003. *Mortal Stakes: Hunters and Hunting in Contemporary America*. Boston: University of Massachusetts Press.

Enloe, Cynthia. 2000. *Maneuvers: The International Politics of Militarizing Women's Lives*. Berkeley/Los Angeles: University of California Press.

Farr, Vanessa, Hernir Myrttinen, and Albrecht Schnabel, eds. 2009. *Sex Pistols: The Gendered Impact of Small Arms and Light Weapons*. Toyko/New York/Paris: United Nations University Press.

Feitz, Lindsey and Joane Nagel. 2008. "The Militarization of Gender and Sexuality in the Iraq War." Pp. 201–225 in *Women in the Military and in Armed Conflict*, eds. C.H. Carreiras and G. Kümmel. Heidelberg, Germany: VS Verlag.

Fenner, Lorry M., and Marie E. deYoung. 2001. *Women in Combat: Civic Duty or Military Liability?* Washington, DC: Georgetown University Press.

Francke, Linda Bird. 1997. *Ground Zero: The Gender Wars in the Military*. New York, NY: Simon & Schuster.

Gallup Poll. 2009. "Gun Ownership and Use in America." Retrieved July 15, 2011 (http://www.gallup.com/poll/20098/gun-ownership-use-america.aspx).

Gibbs, Nancy. 2010. "Sexual Assaults on Female Soldiers: Don't Ask, Don't Tell." *Time* (March 8).

Gossett, Jennifer, and Joyce Williams. 1998. "Perceived Discrimination among Women in Law Enforcement." *Women and Criminal Justice 10*(1): 53–73.

Graebner, Hegwisch, Ariane, and Hannah Liepmann. 2010. "The Gender Wage Gap by Occupation—IWPR." *The Institute for Women's Policy Research—WPR*. Retrieved October 13 (http://www.iwpr.org/publications/pubs/the-gender-wage-gap-by-occupation).

Hennenberger, Melinda. 1993. "NRA Campaign under Attack: The Small Arms Industry Comes On To Women." *New York Times* (Late edition, East Coast) (October 24): A4.

Herbert, Bob. 1994. "The 'Elegant' Handgun." *New York Times* (Late edition) (December 4): 19.

Herbert, Melissa. 1998. *Camouflage Isn't Only for Combat: Gender, Sexuality and Women in the Military*. New York/London: New York University Press.

Holm, Jeannie. 1982. *Women in the Military: An Unfinished Revolution*. New York: Presidio Press.

Homsher, Deborah. 2001. *Women & Guns: Politics and the Culture of Firearms in America*. Armonk, New York: M.E. Sharpe. (Expanded edition with primary source material.)

Honey, Maureen. 1984. *Creating Rosie the Riveter: Class, Gender and Propaganda during WW2*. Amherst: University of Massachusetts Press.

Izraeli, Dafna. 2000. "Gendering Military Service in the Israeli Defense Forces." Pp. 203–26 in *A Soldier and a Woman: Sexual Integration in the Military*, eds. Gerard DeGroot and Corinna Peniston Bird. Harlow, U.K.: Longman.

Jackson, Louise A. 2006. *Women Police, Gender, Welfare and Surveillance in the Twentieth Century*. Manchester/New York: Manchester University Press.

Jacobs, Ron. 1997. *The Way the Wind Blew: A History of the Weather Underground*. London/New York: Verso Press.

Janda, Lance. 2000. "A Simple Matter of Equality: The Admission of Women to West Point." Pp. 305–19 in *A Soldier and a Woman: Sexual Integration in the Military*, eds. Gerard DeGroot and Corinna Peniston Bird. Harlow, U.K.: Longman.

Jans, Nick. 2011. "What Palin's Show Says About Us." *USA Today* (January 5): News/Opinion section.

Jeffreys, Sheila. 2007. "Double Jeopardy: Women, the US Military and the War in Iraq." *Women's Studies International Forum* 30(1): 16–25.

Jones, Joseph. 2009. "In U.S., Record-Low Support for Stricter Gun Laws." *Gallup Poll*, Princeton, NJ, October 9.

Kelly, Caitlin. 2004. *Blown Away: American Women and Guns*. New York, NY: Simon & Schuster.

Kleykamp, Meredith A. 2007. "Military Service as a Labor Market Outcome." *Race, Gender & Class* 14(3–4): 65–69, 72–76.

Langton, Lynn. 2010. "Women in Law Enforcement, 1987–2008." *Bureau of Justice Statistics (BJS)* June 21. Retrieved October 13, 2011 (http://bjs.ojp.usdoj.gov/index.cfm?ty=pbdetail).

LeBlanc-Ernest, Angela D. 1998. "The Most Qualified Person to Handle the Job: Black Panther Party Women, 1966–1982." Pp. 305–36 in *The Black Panther Party Reconsidered*, ed. Charles E. Jones. Baltimore, MD: The Black Classic Press.

Levin, Dana. S. 2011. "You're Always First a Girl." *Journal of Adolescent Research* 26(1): 3–29.

Los Angeles Police Department. "Join LAPD: Salary." *Police Jobs with Los Angeles Police Department*. Retrieved October 1, 2011 (http://www.joinlapd.com/salary.html).

Lumsden, Linda. 2009. "Good Mother's with Guns: Framing Black Womanhood in the Black Panthers, 1968–1980." *Journalism & Mass Communication Quarterly* 86(4) (Winter): 900–22.

McCrum, Lindsay. 2011. *Chicks with Guns*. New York: The Vendome Press.

McIntyre, Ben. 2000. "You Can't Mess with a Million Moms." *The Times* (May 12).

Maze, Rick. 2011. "Bill Would Ease Compensation for Sexual Trauma." Retrieved May 15, 2012 (http://www.armytimes.com/news/2011/03/military-sexual-assault-trauma-veterans-compensation-030811w).

Meyer, Leisa. 1998. *Creating G.I. Jane: Sexuality and Power in the Women's Army Corps during World War II*. New York: Columbia University Press.

Miller, Laura. 1998. "Feminism and the Exclusion of Army Women from Combat." *Gender Issues* 16(3): 33–65.

Moon, Katharine H. S. 1999. "Military Prostitutes and the Hypersexualization of Militarized Women." Pp. 209–24 in *Gender Camouflage*. New York: New York University Press.

Moskos, Charles. 2000. *The Postmodern Military*. New York/Oxford: Oxford University Press.

Mothers' Arms. "Mother's Arms." *Mother's Arms—Protecting What's Ours*. Retrieved July 1, 2011 (http://www.mothersarms.org/faq.html).

Nagel, Joane and Feitz, Lindsey. 2007. "Deploying Race, Gender, Class & Sexuality in the Iraq War." *Race, Gender & Class: An Interdisciplinary Journal* 14: 28–30, 34–47.

National Institute of Justice. (November 2000). "Full Report of the Prevalence, Incidence, and Consequences of Violence against Women: Findings from the National Violence against Women Survey/National Institute of Justice." *National Institute of Justice: Criminal Justice Research, Development and Evaluation*. Retrieved September 13, 2011 (http://www.nij.gov/pubs-sum/183781.htm).

New York Police Department. "Benefits and Salary Overview." Retrieved October 1, 2011 (http://nypdrecruit.com/benefits-salary/overview).

Peniston Bird, Corinna. 2000. "Delilah Shaves Her Hair: Women, the Military and Hollywood." Pp. 320–36 in *A Soldier and A Woman: Sexual Integration in the Military*, eds. Gerard J. DeGroot and Corinna Peniston Bird. Harlow, U.K.: Longman.

Population Bulletin. 2004. "America's Military Population." *59*(4).

Potter, Claire Bond. 1995. " 'I'll Go the Limit and Then Some': Gun Molls, Desire, and Danger in the 1930s." *Feminist Studies 21*(1) (Spring): 41–66.

Rand, Michael, and Jennifer Truman. 2010 (October 3). "Criminal Victimization, 2009." Retrieved 15 September 2011 (http://bjs.ojp.usdoj.gov/index.cfm?ty=pbdetail&iid=2217).

San Francisco Police Department. "San Francisco Police Department: Duties, Salary and Benefits." Retrieved October 1, 2011 (http://sf-police.org/index.aspx?page=1655).

Sanborn, James K. 2012. "USMC-4-Star: Women to attend Infantry School." Posted online April 18. Retrieved May 10, 2012 (http://www.militarytimes.com/news/2012/04/marine-corps-women-infantry-combat-dunford-amos-041812).

Schickel, Richard, Elizabeth Bland, Sally B. Donnellly, and Marth Smilgis. 1991. "Gender Bender over Thelma & Louise." *Time* (June 24).

Second Amendment Sisters. "About Us." Retrieved July 1, 2011 (http://www.2asisters.org/index.php?option=com_content&view=category&id=31:about&Itemid=41&layout=default).

Segal, David R., and Mady W. Segal. 2004 (December). "America's Military Population—Population Reference Bureau." Retrieved July 1, 2011 (http://www.prb.org/Publications/PopulationBulletins/2004/AmericasMilitaryPopulationPDF627KB.aspx).

Sheley, Joseph, Charles J. Brody, and James Wright. 1994. "Women and Handguns: Evidence from National Surveys, 1973–1991." *Social Science Research 23*: 219–35.

Silva, Jennifer. 2008. "A New Generation of Women?" How Female ROTC Cadets Negotiate the Tension between Masculine Military Culture and Traditional Femininity." *Social Forces 87*(2) (December): 937–60.

Singh, Nikhil Pal. 1998. "The Black Panthers and the 'Undeveloped Country' of the Left." Pp. 57–108 in *The Black Panther Party Reconsidered*, ed. Charles E. Jones. Baltimore: Black Classic Press.

Smith, Emily. 2008. *The Sun*, p. 8.

Smith, Tom W., and Robert J. Smith. 1995. "Changes in Firearms Ownership among Women, 1980–1994." *Journal of Criminal Law and Criminology 86*: 133–49.

Smith & Wesson. "Smith & Wesson Firearms." Retrieved July 15, 2011 (http://www.smith-wesson.com/webapp/wcs/stores/servlet/CustomContentDisplay?langId=-1&storeId=750001&catalogId=750051&content=11001).

Standifer, Cid. 2012. "All Services Will Set Up Sexual Assault SUVs." Posted on Tuesday, April 17 at 9:47:43 EST. Retrieved June 20, 2012 (http://www.militarytimes.com/news/2012/04/military-panetta-all-services-sexual-assault-prevention-svu-041712w).

Stange, Mary Zeiss, and Carol K. Oyster. 2000a. *Gun Women: Firearms and Feminism in Contemporary America*. New York/London: New York University Press.

———. 2000b. "High Noon at the Gender Gap: Feminism and the Firearms Debate." P. 21 in *Firearms and Feminism in Contemporary America*. New York/London: New York University Press.

Summerfield, Penny. 2000. "She Wants a Gun not a Dishcloth: Gender, Service and Citizenship in Britain in the Second World War." Pp. 119–34 in *A Soldier and A Woman: Women in the Military*, eds. Gerald J. DeGroot and Corinna Peniston Bird. Harlow, U.K.: Longman.

Tjaden, Patricia, and Nancy Thoennes (US Department of Justice). 2000. *Full Report of the Prevalence, Incidence and Consequences of Violence against Women*. Washington, DC: Office of Justice Programs, National Institute of Justice.

The Learning Channel (TLC). "Sarah Palin's Alaska: TLC." Aired November 14, 2010–January 9, 2011. Retrieved July 15, 2011 (http://tlc.howstuffworks.com/tv/sarah-palins-alaska).

United States Army. 2010 (September 30). "Army Profiles (FY 10)-Tri Fold." Retrieved June 1, 2011 (http://www.armyg1.army.mil/hr/docs/demographics/FY10_Army_Profile.pdf).

Varon, Jeremy. 2004. *Bringing the War Home: The Weather Underground, The Red Army Faction, and Revolutionary Violence in the Sixties and Seventies*. Berkeley/Los Angeles/London: University of California Press.

Walsh, Sean Collins. 2001. "Sex Assaults Underreported, Inquiry into V.A. Concludes." *New York Times* (Late edition, East Coast) (June 9): A16.

Washington Post. 2008. "Editorial." (Late edition) (August 8): A16.

Weissert, Will. 2012. "MTI Receives 20-year-sentences in Sex Assaults." Retrieved May 28, 2012 (www.thearmytimes.com/news/2012/07/ap-air-force-san-antonio-lackland-20-year-sentence-assaults-072112).

Williams, Christine. 1995. *Still A Man's World: Men Who Do Women's Work*. Berkeley/Los Angeles/London: University of California Press.

Williams, Kayla. 2005. *Love My Rifle More Than You: Young and Female in the U.S. Army*. New York/London: W.W. Norton.

Winkler, Adam. 2011. *Gunfight: The Battle over the Right to Bear Arms in America*. New York/London: W.W. Norton.

Yuval-Davis, Nira. 1985. "Front and Rear: The Sexual Division of Labor in the Israeli Army." *Feminist Studies 11*(3) (Fall): 649–75.

Glossary/Index

A

Abron, JoNina M. 16

Acker, Joan 36, 53

advertisements for firearms 2–3, 8, 9

Afghanistan 48, 70, 71

    sexual assaults on women in 61, 62, 63, 64, 65

age structure in U.S. military 54

American Civil Liberties Union (ACLU) 64

B

Benedict, Helen 60, 61, 64, 65, 66

Berger, Dan 19

Black Panther Party for Self Defense: an urban Black political party founded in Oakland, California in October of 1966 by Huey Newton and Bobby Seale who met as community college students. The Black Panther Party, a Black Leftist political group, was established in response to the police brutality, violence, and racism directed specifically towards Black people in Oakland, California. It expanded and became a national party with chapters in Chicago and other cities and was distinguished by its emphasis upon political education, anti-hunger programs (free breakfast), and anti-poverty programs. The Black Panthers redefined the meaning of citizenship for Black people who had been denied their civil rights for a century in the United States since emancipation from slavery. 15, 16–18, 20

Blacks in U.S. army 44

Black women

    armed 16, 17, 18

    gun ownership among 30, 32

    lack of access to gun training 30

    lifetime risk of homicide 31

    similarities with White frontier women of past 31–32

    in U.S. army 30

    views on gun control 32

Blauner, Robert 20
Blown Away (book by Caitlin Kelly) 9
Botti, David 62, 63, 65
Brody, Charles 8–9
Browder, Laura 2, 3, 9, 15, 21, 42
Brown, Elaine 16, 17
Bulmillier, Elisabeth 63

C
Cantu, Cassandra 64
Chavez, Dennis 38
Chicago police 19
Christoffersen, John 64–65
clothing strategies of military women 50
Cointelpro *see* **Counter Intelligence Program**
combat positions 36, 53–54, 70
    banning of women from 41, 42–43, 52, 54
    blurring of line between non-combatant and 54, 70
    and links to pay and promotion 52, 53, 54, 68
command rape: this term refers to the rape or sexual assault of female soldiers by men who are either their "commanding officers" or are superior to them in rank. Female soldiers who are ordered to appear at the room of a commanding officer can be coerced into sex or forcibly raped and typically have little recourse since the chain of command includes the person who sexually assaulted them. If a woman refuses to engage in coercive sex with a male superior her career can be jeopardized, she could be dishonorably discharged, punished, ostracized by fellow soldiers, and her life put at risk. 61
Commission on the Status of Women: established in 1960 by President John F. Kennedy to collect data on the condition of women. This commission, which was headed by Eleanor Roosevelt, the widow of former President Franklin Delano Roosevelt, documented widespread systematic discrimination against women in employment. These forms of discrimination were legal. The report of this commission led to the Equal Pay Act of 1963. 38
conscription *see* **draft**
Counter Intelligence Program: operated by the FBI beginning in the 1950s, known by the acronym Cointelpro , the Counter Intelligence Program was a covert operation that employed and incited extralegal violence among and against members of civil rights organizations, anti-war student groups, revolutionary political groups, and social justice groups 19
Creating G.I. Jane 43, 44

crime, Gallup survey on 7
criminal records 65–66
Crow, Eli Painted 64

D
Dalesio, Emery P. 60
Debray, Regis 21
Dees-Thomases, Donna 26, 27
Defense Advisory Committee on Women in the Services (DACOWITS): created in
1951 by Congress as an advisory arm to the Pentagon and an advocacy organiza-
tion during the Korean War 39
DeGroot, Gerard 52
Democrats 7, 38, 68
Department of Defense: in the United States this is also referred to as The Pentagon,
a reference to the shape of the building where the Department of Defense head-
quarters are located in Virginia 39, 70
mishandling sexual assault and rape cases 60–61, 65
reports on sexual assaults 49, 62
sued by ACLU 64
de Young, Marie 41
Dirk, Kirby (producer of documentary film *The Invisible War*) 60
District of Columbia v. Heller 33
Dizard, Jan 10
Dohrn, Bernadine 18, 19, 20
draft: the civic obligation (for male citizens) to serve in the military for a specified period
of time. Until 1973 men between the ages of 17 and 35 were required to register for
the "draft," a lottery system in which men could be called up to go to war. The draft
was ended in 1973 and the U.S. Armed Forces shifted to an All-Volunteer Army. 40

E
Enloe, Cynthia 40, 41, 47–48
Equal Pay Act 1963 38

F
family benefits in U.S. military 56, 57–58
Feitz, Lindsey 45, 46, 62
female soldiers
combatant status of 53–54
comparison between United States and Israel 52–53
cultural myths about 42–47

mothers as 56–57

negotiating femininity and sexuality 47–51

numbers on active duty 2010 56

percentage in U.S. military 40

permanent place in army for 38–40

positions and occupations open to 49

race/ethnicity of 51

recruitment in All-Volunteer Army 40–41

femininity

central to military training in 1960s 38, 39

clothing and physical appearance in managing of 47, 51

a comparative analysis 52–53

as incompatible with being a soldier 51

media representations of 44, 46

negotiating sexuality and 47–51

feminism: this term originated during the European enlightenment. In the mid-19th century in Europe, women and men began to organize and fight for the rights of women to be treated as full citizens (e.g. to own property in their own names, to vote, to run for elected office, to have access to the same educational opportunities as men). This term refers to the fact that women are systematically oppressed and discriminated against as a group and, therefore, there is a need to advocate on behalf of women in order to end discrimination based upon one's sex role. Feminism has many varieties (liberal, Black, Marxist, cultural, etc.) and encompasses women of diverse racial/ethnic, religious, and class backgrounds. 1, 8, 26, 38, 40, 69–70

Fenner, Lorry 40

"First Defense" program 29–30

Francke, Linda Bird 58

Frattaroli, Shannon 32

free men: this term refers to men who were not enslaved (as most Africans and U.S.-born people of any recognizable African or multiracial ancestry were) and, if legally classified and recognized as "White," were not held as "indentured servants" (paying off their debts for a limited period of time through their labor) and were thus entitled to participate as full citizens in the recently formed United States 14

frontier women 1, 31–32

G

Gallup Polls 6–7

gender: legal status as a woman or man, usually based on sex assignment at birth. Gender status (as opposed to biological sex) is responsible for the social production of patterns for social expectations for bodies, behavior, emotions, family, and work roles. For example, women are assumed and expected to be more nurturing and thus better suited for jobs such as nursing, childcare, and not ideally suited for occupations that require the use of lethal weapons or that are associated with masculinity such as fighting fires, security, and construction work. 1

gender camouflage: the practice of concealing one's sex and gender in order to pass as a social male to serve in the military. This was not uncommon among women who wanted to serve in the all-male military during the Revolutionary War. The assumptions about women's appropriate gender roles was so powerful that, in many cases, male soldiers did not even suspect that their comrades were anatomical females until after they had given birth. 37–38

gender display: presentation of self as a gendered person through the use of markers or symbols such as clothing, hairstyles, jewelry. Managing interactions with others using behavior and physical activities considered appropriate for one's sex. 50

gendered barriers/gendered boundaries (see also **gender segregation**): an obstacle that was created by institutional policies and translates into horizontal segregation by gender, that is women are concentrated in different occupations within the military, and vertical segregation (women are concentrated in the lower levels of administration and pay grades due to their failure to advance). In other words, there are still fewer opportunities for women to move into leadership roles and to earn as much as men in salary and pension benefits. For example, until 2012, women were barred from training in Quantico, Virginia, where the Infantry Battalion combat leaders are trained. 16, 42, 54, 70

gendered division of labour: the assignment of jobs and social roles based on one's sex 42

gendered institution: Joan Acker, a feminist sociologist, uses this term to describe the way that gender inequalities are reflected in an organizational structure. The processes, practices, images, and ideologies and distributions of power in the various sectors of social life are organized along gender lines and reflect gender inequalities. Some institutions such as the Catholic priesthood, men's prisons, all-male academies, and athletic clubs are defined by the absence of women. 36, 53

gendered violence 69–71

gender equality 37, 38, 52, 58, 68

gender gap: this concept was originally used to describe differences in female and male voting behavior in political elections including votes for candidates, political party preferences, and policy preferences. Between 1920 when women were granted the right to vote and 1980 there were few differences between White male and female voters in their political party preferences. This changed in 1980 with the election of Ronald Reagan, who was more popular with men than with women. In 1982 the gap widened between female and male voters with women showing a strong preference for Democratic candidates. This term is now also used to refer to economic differences between women and men, that is gender inequalities in pay, salaries, and access to resources. 6–7

gender ideologies: socially sanctioned beliefs about what are appropriate and acceptable male and female roles. The idea that combat is an exclusively masculine activity and that heroism is reserved for men is a gender ideology that has been enforced through specific military policies, formal and informal practices. 37, 39, 42, 54

gender integration 40

gender regime: an institutional arrangement that produces social inequalities in the positions that men and women occupy and in their interactions 53

gender segregation: this refers to the concentration of men and women in different sectors, occupations, and workplaces. The idea of occupational segregation was originally developed under Dual Labor Market theories (later called Segmented Labor Market theories) to explain why the wage rates of Black American men consistently lagged behind those of White men's but it was then applied to White women's employment. 42, 69, 70

Gibbs, Nancy 63

Graebner, Ariane 22

Gulf War: this war took place between August 1990 and March 1991 and was fought with the support of 40,000 women deployed to Saudi Arabia. More American women fought in a war zone during the Gulf War than had fought in any American war since World War II (see Enloe 1994: 81). 53–54

gun magazines 9

gun molls: young White women, usually U.S. born, who grew up on rural farms and migrated to the urban cities like Chicago to work. They established romantic, sexual, and kinship relationships with men who were engaged in criminal activities that could include kidnapping, bank robberies, contract murders, protection rackets, and gun smuggling or running. J. Edgar Hoover began to target these women for arrest and conviction in 1934. A famous example is Bonnie Parker of the infamous Bonnie and Clyde team of bank robbers. 12–14

gun ownership

    Black Panthers claims for African American 17

    entwined with citizenship and gender inequality 6, 7

    feminist opposition to women's 26

    gender gap in 6–7

    highest in safest neighborhoods 33

    levels of 7, 9

    meaning of 10

    media portrayals of 8, 9, 28

    modern-day women and 3–6

    race and 7, 14, 17, 30–31, 32

    reasons for 8, 9, 10

    regional disparities for women in gun violence and 32

unable to defend women from intimate or gendered violence 66, 69

White nationalism and 10, 14–16

gun regulation debate 25–26

Blacks more likely to support control than Whites 31–32

District of Columbia v. Heller 33

and empowering of women argument 33–34

Gallup poll surveys and public views on 7

Million Moms March 26–27

National Rifle Association 27

Safely in Mother's Arms 28–30

gun safety, teaching women and children 28–30

gun violence 31, 33

Gun Women 26

H

Hearst, Patricia Campbell: born in 1954, Patty Hearst was kidnapped in 1974 while she was an art student at UC-Berkeley. She became a fugitive after participating in a bank robbery in San Francisco. An heiress and the daughter of William Hearst, the editor of the *San Francisco Chronicle*, she became the most famous White female armed dissident of her era. President Bill Clinton gave her a full pardon on January 20, 2001. 22–23

and Symbionese Liberation Army 22–23

Hendrie, Alison 27

Henneberry, Chantelle 64

Herbert, Bob 9

Herbert, Melissa 50–51

heritage hunters: a term that I use to refer to women and men who "inherit" their passion for hunting and their gun training as children. Hunting is a "tradition" in their family and it is passed down to them from parents or other family members. The experience of hunting is routine, ritualized, and often occurs in rural areas. 10

Holm, Jennie 38–39, 39–40, 41

homicide, lifetime risk of 31

Homsher, Deborah 25, 28, 31–32

I

internal colonialism, theory of 20

intimate partner: a person with whom you live, cohabit, and/or who has access to your home 34

intimate partner violence: the most common form of sexual assault and violence against women involves their husbands, domestic spouses, partners, and other individuals with whom they have a close relationship 33, 34, 66, 69

The Invisible War: a 2012 documentary by Kirby Dirk and Amy Ziering which premiered at the Sundance Film Festival. This documentary investigates the experiences of female soldiers who are "military rape" survivors. We meet several women and their family members from various branches of the U.S. Armed Services including the Army, the Marines, and the Coast Guard. It calls attention to a masculine culture which has failed to take seriously sexual violence and instead has tended to punish women who come forward and report their experiences. After seeing a screening of this film, Leon Panetta, the Secretary of Defense, announced major policy changes including the establishment of "Special Victim Units" (SVUs) in every service (Army, Navy, Marines, Air Force, Coast Guard) which did not previously exist and would handle rape and sexual assault. 60–61, 71
Iraq 48, 71
    sexual assaults on women in 61, 62, 63, 64, 65
Israel comparative analysis of militarized femininity with United States 52–53
Izraeli, Dafna 52, 53

J
Jacobs, Ron 19, 20
Jans, Nick 5
Johnson, Shoshana 45–46

K
Kelly, Caitlin 9, 32, 33, 37–38
Kennedy, President John F. 38
Klay, Ariana 61

L
Lady Smith handgun 8
Laurean, Cesar 60
Lauterbach, Maria 60
leadership of U.S. armed services 36, 70
    promotions linked to holding of combat positions 53, 54, 68, 70
    women underrepresented in 66, 68, 69
LeBlanc-Ernest, Angela 17
legislation, gun 14–15, 16–17, 33
Lewis, Tarika
    and the Black Panther Party 17
Looking For A Few Good Moms 26
Love My Rifle More Than You (memoir by female veteran) 48–49
Lumsden, Linda 17, 18
Lynch, Jessica 45–46

M

McIntyre, Ben 27

Marine Corps Infantry Training Battalions School: This school trains Marines who will be eligible to serve as combat officers. In 2012 it admitted its first female students. This was a major policy change. 70

Marine Corps Times 70

market for guns 8, 31

    excluding women without sufficient resources 30–31, 34

    women's 7–10

masculinity

    guns a symbol of 3, 4, 6, 8, 36

    military service tied to 37, 39, 41, 45

maternalism: this refers to the use of women's status as "mothers" and their "moral" capital as nurturers to effect political change and assert a political voice as citizens 27

media

    images of women in Gulf War 53

    portrayals of women and gun ownership 8, 9, 28

    representations of female soldiers 44–47

Meyer, Lisa 43–44, 44–45

military academy 38

military industrial complex 52

military sexual trauma (MST): a form of psychological trauma that is a direct result of sexual assault, sexual harassment, or unwanted sexual activity that occurred while on active duty. This includes rape, attempted rape, sexual harassment, or any other unwanted sexual contact or activity. 49, 61, 64, 65, 66, 68

Military Times 60, 64–65

Million Mom March: a mass demonstration organized by Donna Dees-Thomases, a mother, in support of increased federal regulation of gun sales that occurred on May 14, 2000, which was Mother's Day. An estimated 500,000 people participated which made it the largest political demonstration held in Washington, DC since the Vietnam War. 26–28

moral waivers 65–66

Mortal Stakes 10

mothers, attraction of military for 56–57

murder of a woman Marine 60

N

Nagel, Joane 45, 46, 62

nationalism and gun ownership 10, 14–16

National Rifle Association 4, 8, 27

    women's division 8

New Left 19, 20–21, 22
Newsweek 62
Newton, Huey 16, 17, 18

O

Oakley, Annie: born Phoebe Ann Moses in 1860 in rural Ohio, she later adopted the stage name of Annie Oakley. In 1887, while performing in Buffalo Bill Cody's Wild West Show, she became the most famous female exhibition or "target" shooter in U.S. history. As a White married woman who wore her hair long and never wore pants, she cultivated a feminine and anti-feminist image despite superior skills that enabled her to beat men much older. Although Oakley lived during the first wave of feminism she did not support gender equality or women's right to vote and distanced herself from feminist activists. 1–2

occupational segregation: men work in occupations carried out primarily by other men such as construction work, firefighting, truck driving, and surgery, while women work in jobs carried out primarily by women such as childcare, nursing, primary school teaching, social work, and beauty therapy 38

Oyster, Carol K. 6, 26, 36

P

Palin, Sarah 4–6, 10
Panetta, Leon 61, 68, 70
Peniston Bird, Corinna 52
Piestewa, Lori 45, 46
Pingree, Chellie 68, 69
police brutality
    and Chicago Police Department 19
political dissidents, women 14, 19, 20–21
posttraumatic stress disorder (PTSD) 61, 65
Potter, Claire 12, 13–14
promotions in armed services 52, 53, 54, 68
Public Law 90–130 39–40

R

race
    and gun ownership 7, 14–16, 17, 31, 32
    and media treatment of female soldiers captured/killed 45–47
racial discrimination in workplace 57
racial oppression 20
racism, state sanctioned 16, 18
Radical Oppression in America 20

rape: forced sexual intercourse including both psychological coercion as well as physical force. Forced sexual intercourse means penetration by the offender's penis. It includes attempted and/or completed rapes, male as well as female victims, and both heterosexual and homosexual rapes. 33, 60–61

    culture pervading military 63, 65–66, 71

    problems with reporting 61, 63, 69

Republican Party 4, 5, 6, 7

residential treatment facility for female veterans 61

right to bear arms 15–16, 17

S

Safely in Mother's Arms: an organization founded in 2000 by Alicia Waldas, the White mother of three children, to provide women with training in how to safely and effectively use firearms. It was founded in response to a wave of mass shootings and gun violence perpetuated by White males. According to Ms. Waldas, this organization has members in 36 states. 28–30

salary by rank in U.S. army 43

Samson, Deborah 37–38

school shootings 25, 27, 29

Seale, Bobby 16, 17, 18

semiotics: the study of signs and their use in social life. A sign uses a signifier such as a word or an image in order to represent a mental image that we have of an idea, an object, or an image (the signified). For example, the image of a White woman holding a gun may signify a very different idea (message) from that of a Black woman wearing her hair natural (in an Afro) pointing a gun, depending upon the viewer and the historical context. The same word or image (sign) can signal different meanings. 17

sex segregation 36, 54

sexual assault: a wide range of victimizations, separate from rape or attempted rape. These crimes include attacks or attempted attacks generally involving unwanted sexual contact between victim and offender. May or may not involve force and can include such actions as grabbing and fondling. It also includes verbal threats. 34, 48, 60–65

    changes to military policy to address 61, 63, 68–69

    higher risk among female soldiers than among civilian peers 61, 66, 70

    institutional barriers to reporting of 68

    in Iraq and Afghanistan 61, 62, 63, 64, 65

    reluctance to report 62, 64

    underreporting of 63, 65

sexuality, negotiating femininity and 47–50

sexual trauma *see* **military sexual trauma (MST)**

Shely, Joseph 8–9

Silva, Jennifer 51

Singh, Nikhil Pal 18

slavery 15, 20

Smith & Wesson
    and women's gun market 7–8, 30
    use of feminist rhetoric to sell small arms 8

Special Victims Units (SVUs): established in April 2012 by Secretary of Defense Leon Panetta to coordinate, collect, store, and manage all reported sexual assault cases, this is a centralized database that will serve all branches of the U.S. Armed Forces 68–69, 71

Stange, Mary Zeiss 6, 26, 36

Students for a Democratic Society (SDS): a student organization founded in 1960 at the University of Michigan. At its peak it had 100,000 members. In 1968 they elected Bernardine Dohrn, a 25-year-old native of Chicago, as its national leader. 18–19, 21

suffrage: the right to vote. Women in the United States did not receive the right to vote (at the federal level) until 1920. Most Black women were prevented from voting until the late 1960s. 1

Summerfield, Penny 39, 42, 54

Symbionese Liberation Army 22, 23

T

target shooting, women 1–2, 3, 4, 10

A Taste for Power 16, 17

Taurus Marketing 8

The Times 27

Title VII of the 1964 Civil Rights Act 68

"typewriter soldiers" 38–39

U

Uniform Military Code of Justice 61, 68

Uniform Militia Act of 1792: this Act required free able-bodied White males between the ages of 18 and 45 to enroll in a militia, bearing their own arms and equipment, but it banned from service all slaves, freed Blacks, and Indians 15

uniforms 47

United States Military Academy: commonly known as "West Point," was established in 1802 to provide training and education for men who would become officers and assume the leadership roles in the U.S. Army. Women were denied admission to West Point until 1976, more than 174 years after it was established. 36

V

Varon, Jeremy 21

Veterans' National Center for Posttraumatic Stress Disorder 61

Victorian era: a historical period that takes its name from Queen Victoria who sat on the British throne (1837–1901). Several forms of popular culture emerged in the United States during this time which consolidated White supremacy and White nationalism among European immigrants and European Americans from diverse cultural, linguistic, ethnic, and religious backgrounds. One form was the Wild West shows, the precursor to the "Western" film genre in which White people and cowboys were portrayed as "heroic" and White women were first seen as domestic gunslingers. 1–3, 20, 21

Vietnam War: a Cold War conflict that involved the U.S. military for two decades. Between 1955 and 1973 the U.S. military was involved in what it defined as an anti-Communist takeover of South Vietnam. Although the United States ended its involvement in August of 1973 the Vietnam War officially ended with the fall of Saigon in April of 1975. 20, 21

W

Waldas, Alicia (founder of Safely in Mother's Arms) 28–30

Washington Post 33, 38

weapons training, military 36, 41, 43–44, 66

Weatherman (Weather Underground): an offshoot of Students for a Democratic Society, and a New Left radical political organization founded in 1968. The name of the Weatherman is taken from a Bob Dylan song titled "Subterranean Blues" that was released in 1963. This group, in contrast to most of the New Left political groups, advocated violence as a necessary strategy to counter U.S. imperialism, racism, and capitalism and the violence of the U.S. government which targeted progressive anti-Vietnam and anti-racist groups. It became one of the most well known New Left groups due to its embrace of violence as a legitimate response to U.S. imperialism. 19–20, 21

Wild West shows 1–2

Williams, Kayla 48–49

Winkler, Adam 14, 15

Women and Guns 28

Women's Armed Services Act 1948 38

Wright, James 8–9

Z

Ziering, Amy 60

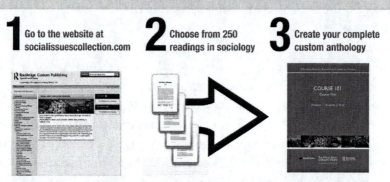